T0392248

SHRIKRISHNA KASHYAP:

A Master
On the Liberating Power of Dignity

SHRIKRISHNA KASHYAP:

A Master
On the Liberating Power of Dignity

Compiled and Edited by
Patricia Brown, PhD (Gayatri)

SHRIKRISHNA KASHYAP: A MASTER

iUniverse books may be ordered through booksellers or by contacting:

iUniverse
1663 Liberty Drive
Bloomington, IN 47403
www.iuniverse.com
1-800-Authors (1-800-288-4677)

ISBN: 978-1-5320-4134-1 (sc)
ISBN: 978-1-5320-4136-5 (e)

Library of Congress Control Number: 2018900807

Print information available on the last page.

iUniverse rev. date: 02/24/2018

Other books and CDs by Wisdom Wave, Inc., Santa Fe, New Mexico are as follows.

Wisdom Wave Books:
Little Book of the Self: Jewels in the Crown of Self Realization, S. Kashyap & Gayatri
The Shoreless Ocean, S. Kashyap
The Supplicate Order: An Invocation of the Sacred, Gayatri
A Wave Named Blue (children's book), Gayatri

Wisdom Wave CDs:
Satyam Shivam Sundaram, S. Kashyap and Friends
Shyam Sings: Solos by S. Kashyap
Ave: A Folk Opera of the Two Marys, a Musical, Gayatri
Mundo Tercero (Third World), a Musical, Gayatri

Web site: www.wisdomwave.org
Wisdomwave80@gmail.com (505) 455-2268

Shyam is Shyam. God is God.
The twains always meet.

This is the era of emancipation from all the shortcomings.

SHRIKRISHNA KASHYAP (DR. SHYAM)

Figure 1

It is incorrect to say, "I made a choice." That is a corruption of happiness. Love is not a choice. Love is not superficial. To go above ignorance is not making a choice. Perfect happiness is the absence of happiness. It is flowing life.

Loving Memorials from Friends

(In order received)

Since 1973, dear master Shyam has been guiding my life from Rishikesh, Bombay, and Lonavla, Brazil and at distance, from Santa Fe, forty-two years on the physical plane and now from wherever he dwells. Wisdom, humility, compassion, patience, love, nobility, and brotherhood were the best spirituality enhancing lessons given by him. I wish to be worthy of my Divine master's precious teachings.

Premdas - Jak Pilozof; Nucleo de Yoga Center, Belo Horizonte, Brazil

Bodies die, but genuine wisdom doesn't. Dr. Shyam made the world a better place, and his wisdom continues to do so.

Larry Dossey, MD; Author: *ONE MIND: How Our Mind Is Part of a Greater Consciousness and Why It Matters*; and many more

The one thing I recall he said to us and also to the group had to do with reading books and not living what we learned. Don recalled his time as an adjunct at OSU in 2002-2003; he would stop by and visit with Shyam on his way back home from class. On one of these occasions Don remarked on how many books he had read over the years and yet not really gleaned as much as he felt he should have. Paraphrasing at this point, Shyam replied, "Perhaps you should put the books down and live your life." This is just one of the many "pearls" Shyam gifted us with over the many years we were privileged to know him... the words of a truly wise and spiritual man. Peace and blessings,

Don and De Crow; Stillwater, Oklahoma

Shyam entered my life
When I thought it would not mend,
He was my brother, my father,
My teacher, my friend.

Tasha Mansfield, PhD; Psychologist, Miami, Florida

Dr. Shyam will always remain close to our hearts. Just about ten years ago, he conducted our marriage and we had the good fortune of sitting in some of his discourses shortly thereafter. His wisdom and compassion is unparalleled. He is a beacon of light that will never diminish.

Erika and Niranjan Seshadri, MD; Sarasota, Florida

Is it not he who is a True Friend the one who shares the path to freedom selflessly with another a Real Friend? So for me, I say Shyam is a True Friend in all ways to all those paths he had crossed, including mine.

Richard Young; Albuquerque, New Mexico

Dear Friends of Shyam of many years standing, Shyam and I discussed the problems of the world, and I was so pleased to be his friend. The world needs to remember the many ways that Shyam helped others, and I hope that someone in the future will follow in his footsteps.

Murray I. Mantell, PhD, Professor Emeritus; Department of Civil Engineering, University of Miami, Miami, Florida

I only had the pleasure of staying with Dr. Shyam one night years ago, but his joyful, simple presence still resonates today as a model of being.

Susanne Cook-Greuter, PhD; www.verticaldevelopment.com

Shyam moved through my memories in a perfectly natural and respectful way. He understood without me having to say anything. He explained without me asking. He brought joy to my heart. He made Ursula laugh. We love him.

Dorothea Smith

He was like a grandfather who could always read my mind.

Ursula Smith

"There's nothing holy about holistic medicine if you don't get a traditional education!" And with those words, Shyam refused to let me into teachings at his house until I had registered at the College of Santa Fe. I owe all of my graduate education to his encouragement. He taught us, fussed at us, supported us, and loved us unconditionally. We are all so blessed to have known him.

Sandra Pope, MPH, PhD

The Light and Love of God lived within his heart. That Light and that Love poured forth to all he met. We are blessed to have known him and have been in his presence.

Susan and Elliott McDowell: www.elliottmcdowell.com

I first knew Dr. Shyam as a healing practitioner both for myself and my daughter. But he gave us much more than his work on our bodies; he also touched our hearts and soul. I have been privileged to hear him teach and to sing with his devotees. I am grateful in the many ways he has touched my life.

Kathleen Magee; Santa Fe, New Mexico

He was a patient weaver of truth in the fire of illumination. He had a total intensity and love for us, in his wanting us to grow and evolve. He said, "We have a spiritual immune system, but we don't know how to use it. "There are so many deep and wonderful things Shyam woke up or sparked inside like his statements: "Where there is gratitude, there is no room for depression," is so powerful. He said, "Choose life in whatever you do. You cannot escape yourself."

Sandra Canzone, DOM; Santa Fe, New Mexico; www.drscanzone.com

It is hard to put into a few sentences a short tribute to my beloved mentor, friend, Ayurvedic physician, and spiritual teacher. The love that I feel for Dr. Shyam transcends any kind of worldly love and my gratitude to him feels boundless. For over 25 years, Shyam provided me with wise counsel, ministered to my body and psyche, and filled my soul with wisdom and faith. His love and guidance will forever be with me in my heart.

Andrea Mantell Seidel, PhD; Professor Emeritus, Dance; Associate Professor, Religious Studies; Florida International University; www.spiritdanceart.org

Shyam's radiant being lit up our lives. Through his boundless generosity, wit, and wisdom, Shyam pushed each of us fortunate to have been in his presence beyond our limited selves - to develop our talents and to spread our colorful wings in this glorious world. He taught me to taste and opened the door to the sacred life. Shyam surely saved my life and he inspires me every day.

> You were our bright, constant star
> Blazing bright and warm until
> The soft snow came with a swirling chill.
> Four weeks later a colder, blowing storm
> Reminded us of your eternal truths
> Shared as a stardust smile.
> Now your visage beams at us
> From an altar honoring your effulgent light.
> Be good, do good – do not be bothered
> By the circumstances of immaterial vicissitudes
> Love generously and enjoy this precious life.

Lynn Walters, PhD; Founder Cooking with Kids, Inc. www.cookingwithkids.org

Shyam - you taught me what it means to believe, that the sun and moon can live in the soul of a human, and that love has no end. I will be good and do good.

Lily Hofstra, MSc

I had asked Dr. Shyam if he would list for me the therapeutic action of a specific Homeopath because the literature often cites multiple uses. His comment was, "If I tell you that this Homeopathic Medicine is only used for specific diseases then you will look no further and therefore never discover for yourself what else the medicine could treat. The use of herbs is not static; it is ever changing, and it is your duty as practitioners to discover their healing qualities."

David Canzone, DOM; Santa Fe, New Mexico; www.drscanzone.com

Shyam taught me that we have something to learn from everyone. He showed me that sometimes a lesson delivered to a crowd is really just for one person. He helped me realize that sometimes saying nothing really is the wisest thing to say.

Keegan Brown, known Shyam as long as he can remember; Full Stack Web Developer; New Orleans, Louisiana; http://mindandcode.com

From my late teens to my early 50's I was blessed to reside in the secure love of my spiritual father, Shyam. With kindness and his unique style of trickster humor along with deep insight and a persistent determination to speak the truth he cajoled me into my better self in every aspect of my life. I truly have learned the attitude of gratitude from him. He is deeply missed.

Brenda Griffiths, MD; Psychiatrist, Canada

Shyam saved my life in many ways. He accentuated service to humanity and the forgotten ones. He inspired the reality of right action in his ability to convey and create greater enthusiasm for the highest good in the everyday life. I have immeasurable gratitude and great love.

Zuleikha; www.storydancer.com; #storydancerproject

Shyam was my brother, and he watched over me from literally the moment I was born. My love for him is as immeasurable as the blessing of having known him.

Komal Chenevert Brown, MPH, MA; New Orleans, Louisiana

Dr. Shyam has been one of my Beloved Teachers for thirty-two years both in and out of the body; A master at extracting your commitment to the Divine, using many methods and individualizing them all for the 100's of people who came to him, he was and is a true healer on the levels it is most needed.

Ananda Magee, MS; Occupational Therapist

In The Presence Of Grace: At my first consultation, I encountered this light being waving his right hand at me in a sweet smelling Zen like room while waves of energy rippled through my body. With a big smile he lowered his hand and said, "So, a bleeding stomach ulcer, can you give up Thanksgiving and Christmas dinner this year?" *Yes,* I replied. Stunned by his para logistic examination, I went to a grocery store to fill my prescription of white potatoes, olive oil, and lemon juice and followed through with his protocol. By January, I was drinking beer without problems. And now, twenty-seven years later, still adhering to an Ayurvedic lifestyle, I remain free of stomach ulcers.

Ralph Steele, MA; Santa Fe, New Mexico; lifetransitiontherapy.com

Shyam is with me all the time, in my heart. I can close my eyes and hear him chant. [We] were so fortunate to have spent so much time with him.

Sundari Ramsayer, PhD Psychologist; Oklahoma City, Oklahoma

Shyam will always be in my heart.

Celeste Miller; Santa Fe, New Mexico

Before I met Shyam, I had been searching for God many years. But when I lost my 17-year-old son to a drunk driver, I felt that my life was over. My wonderful son was gone. I became cold, hard, bitter. Then my beautiful friend Gayatri came into my life, and although I told her I didn't want to meet Shyam, she persisted and finally talked me into meeting him. I literally ran away from him at the end of one of my public talks, and he literally ran after me. At the door, struggling to pull on my boots, I glanced at him. Transfixed by his gaze, the earth moved, the sky opened, and I knew I had met my teacher. He opened my eyes; he opened my heart. When I resisted him, he transformed me. When I turned from the truth, he turned me back to the light. I will love him forever. May God bless this great soul, the source of my joy, my teacher, my friend.

Gabrielle Graham; Santa Fe, New Mexico; www.santafelavender.com

Charming, witty, heart-piercing, no nonsense, and full of love. I remember Shyam as the grandfather I always needed and teacher whose loving care and kindness transcended words; a man in whose eyes I saw the expanse of the universe and the tenderness that healed my heart. Will forever be grateful for your honesty, humor and love, Shyam. Thank you.

Susan MacDonald, M.Ed.; TV Host, Educator and Columnist

Shyam allowed me to see past fear and into faith: faith in God, faith in myself. He was, is, truly Divine. Eternal. And, from him I learned that we are all this, all Divine, all a part of the whole and somehow, whole within our own selves.

Antoinette V. Villamil, MFA; Santa Fe, NM

Although I have been privileged to know and be mentored by many great souls, I have known several who were living Saints, in every aspect of their being, heart, character, and aspiration. Dr. Shyam is a constant inspiration to all that one might be, realize, practice, and hope. Common, yet uncommon. A humble, dignified man, yet ever true and noble. Few people have the courage, modesty, and love to simply become the truth. I have never known Shyam to be anything or anyone but living truth, incarnate.

He taught in two manners which I find profound and holy – he taught that which is possible and good in a person; he taught protecting the vulnerable and holy from that which is violent and not true. He never let the holy fall out of itself, be desecrated. He tended the holiness of life in all that he is, and in all beings, in all of creation, in all of life, in all of reality. A living man as embodiment of the renowned Vedic prayer in Hinduism and South Asian faith traditions – "From the unreal, lead me to the Real."

As an example of the first manner, a woman student once asked him of a mystic and tried to turn him against this person. Shyam stated that this person was real in their practice, abilities, and wishes to help humanity, and that they would continue to deepen in this throughout life.

At Shyam's request of me, I have worked in all ways in which I am able to help all of the people affected by the lineages of a scar of molestation.
Shyam remains and always shall, one of the great blessings of my soul and life. Such an honor to be beside such a Saint. Might I become a worthy daughter of his faith, practice, example, and Heaven's blessing through him.

Elizabeth Anne Hin (Beth); The White Rose Foundation; <u>www.thewhiterose.org</u>

Shrikrishna Kashyap (Dr. Shyam), A Beloved Spiritual Master

Preface

A descendant of a long lineage of ancient *Brahmins*, the priest class of India, Shrikrishna Kashyap (Dr. Shyam) grew up in a small village outside of Mumbai, India. He attained Doctorates in Divinity and in Homeopathic Medicine, but asserted that his real training grew out of his childhood. His paternal grandmother was a well-loved and respected local healer. She would see people coming to their house at some distance down the road and would tell Shyam, as a young boy, to take particular herbs to them before they even reached the house. A deeply devout Brahmin and Yogini, the grandmother would prepare a feast each year, similar to our All Souls' Day here in the United States, for the disembodied seven rishis, considered the progenitors of creation. Sage Kashyap, being the family's ancestor, was among these. As a small boy, Shyam burst into the room seeing these visional beings and sat next to the apparition of his holy forefather who allowed him to share the food! When he was a four-year-old child, Shyam saw a vision of a mantra in the clouds and was told by the family *guru* that he would one day be his own *guru*. Mahatma Gandhi came to his family home, and Shyam sat on his lap. A bit older, he hopped over the wall to see Shri Aurobindo who was in solitude. After a mild scolding by the Mother, Shri Aurobindo gave him an apple from their apple tree by that same wall. When meeting Shri Ramana Maharshi, Shyam was asked, "What do you want?" To this he replied, "I want nothing." At the end of Swami Nityananda's life, he tended to the great saint who died in his arms.

Shyam was a teacher who told the truth to anyone regardless of their station in life. He met Radha Bai as well as Akama Devi, a saint who lived in a cave for fifteen years. She had not eaten that whole time, but Shyam persuaded her to eat. Vishnu Das was another saint/sage who evaded many people. Shyam told him that he had a "right to go anywhere in God's kingdom" and stayed the whole night in a cave with Vishnu Das, who told Shyam he would miss him.

He was also was very close to Shri Anandamayi Ma who loved to make him his favorite treat *gulab jamun*. He warned her once not to ride in a jeep, but she did anyway. The jeep was in an accident and she came back with a splint on her arm, telling him that she should have listened. He would tell her that she needed to take care of her body and not to be so dependent on others. Swami Chidananda asked Ma to attend a festival, but Ma had refused, saying she was ill. Shyam traveled a long distance to her home and entered with a bullock cart full of flowers. She granted him a visit inside her sickroom. Pouring the flowers on her bed, Shyam insisted that she come to the festival. He told her he understood that the spiritual energy was very difficult to handle sometimes. She finally agreed, after getting up and going to the kitchen where she made him *rasgula* sweets with her own hand. Once Ma had a vision of *Krishna* and wanted to build an ashram in Vrindavan. When she was installing statues of *Radha* and *Krishna*, Shyam told her the statues were not correct, his having seen *Krishna* "in reality." During the consecration of the new correctly rendered statues, Ma fainted. Shyam told Didi, Ma's attendant, to take her to her room and bring two *rasgula* sweets to her. When he checked on her, Ma said to him," You are the High Priest, you have to eat," and she put one of the *rasgula* in his mouth. Shyam stated that her "relationship to *Krishna* was purity to purity."

Shrikrishna Kashyap was not only a Brahmin priest but an Eastern Orthodox priest as well with the ancient Antiochian order. He conducted marriage ceremonies for all denominations of people: Hindu, Muslim, Buddhists, and Christians. He even presided over a wedding ceremony in Westminster Abbey for a dear English friend. He also treated the sick in a leper colony, performing eye surgeries and other medical treatments. He helped the patients to make and sell their weavings. He worked tirelessly with the poorest of the poor.

Shyam reported an engaging story about his contact with the Dalai Lama. While the Dalai Lama was building a colony in Northern India, Shyam stayed in a room nearby. Shyam's dog Raja used to bark outside the bedroom door at the Dalai Lama while he snored. One day Raja stole one of the Dalai Lama's sandals, and he couldn't leave. Shyam told Raja to go find the sandal and the beloved dog left and then returned with the missing sandal.

He once recounted his conversation with Jiddu Krishnamurti. He met the exalted world teacher in India along with Dr. David Bohm, the physicist, and also in Los Alamos, New Mexico in 1984, when Krishnamurti gave talks to the national lab on "Creativity and Science." He thought Krishnamurti was omitting an important teaching essential for humanity. Krishnamurti and Dr. Bohm worked out concepts of the implicate and the explicate orders in the cosmos. A subtle sea of fluctuating energy, the implicate order is the hidden unmanifest mystery of quantum "matter," energy, and intelligence. The explicate order is defined as the unfolded forms of the implicate order into manifestation. Dr. Shyam said there is a supplicate order, which is the intermediary medium for human beings with which and through which humans may contact the mysterious unseen. Dr. Shyam insisted that human beings require an intermediate realm with which to contact the unmanifest, which he termed the supplicate order. I later elaborated on this theme in a lengthy work based on years of sitting and learning at his feet.

His profound awakening came after a ninety day fast and recitation of the great *Mahamritanhejaya Mahamantram (Trymbakam),* also recorded on the Wisdom Wave CD *Satyam Shivam Sundaram.* These and many more accounts of his youth and adulthood are written upon our hearts. When he left his cave of enlightenment, Shyam was hounded by throngs of worshipers, but he renounced such acclaim and continued his journey in the world, helping his beloved friend Swami Chidananda to manage the Divine Life Society Ashram in Rishikesh, India, until finally settling in Santa Fe, New Mexico where he taught a few lucky spiritual aspirants, who often and still puzzle as to why he graced us in such a way! His vision of a blue arc of light connecting a mountain in the Himalayas to the Sangre de Christo Mountains in New Mexico guided him to one of his American homes. After moving to Santa Fe, Shyam would see St. Francis of Assisi climbing up and down his home's spiral staircase. His beautiful life was full of majesty, mystery and wonder.

Patricia Brown, PhD (Gayatri) Santa Fe, New Mexico - March, 2017
www.MarysMusical.com
www.WisdomWave.org

Introduction

This book is an outcome of a grieving process for a great being who shared our lives and lifted our spirits. I knew and studied with Dr. Shyam for thirty-three years. Along with two loving and dedicated devotees, Dr. Lynn Walters, PhD and Dr. Sandra Canzone, DOM, we brought his picture to the local Buddhist stupa in Santa Fe and were allowed to place it in the main temple alongside many venerable and revered Lamas of that tradition. Lama Mingma advised us to prepare books commemorating his teachings as a way to give homage to the one who guided us these many years. For a memorial celebration, I began to compile photos of his life, which are shared in this volume, as well as select quotations from profound teachings in *satsangs* (gatherings of truth seekers) he offered since 1980. Of these *satsangs*, he said, "We have steadfastness to the noble cause of realization of oneself. This is an assembly of those with the same aim. Those who do not want to reach this will go."

Dr. Shyam was a remarkable healer of body, mind, and spirit. He is particularly known and appreciated for life changing, wisdom-replete interventions that placed a person firmly and safely on a sane and uplifting path in life. His no-nonsense advice stands in sharp contrast to the contradicting plethora of modernized ancient teachings now saturating the Western world. He said, "I helped many pick up the broken pieces of their lives and go forward into a life of dignity." He stressed the importance of *Sthitaprajna*, to establish oneself in the dignity and steadiness of the Divine Self. Here, he gives us a path and a lifeline from the identity of the ego or the false worldly personality to our birthright, which is united with the universal self.

To reiterate a quote that comes later in this book, he asserted, "People may say, 'My arrogance has saved me.' But it's the dignity that saves. They are not the same thing. If you have dignity, you need not be arrogant at all. You are very humble with simplicity, humility, and humbleness. Dignity maintains everything. Real dignity, not acquired dignity, is your immune system. You conduct yourself with the right behavior, eating the right type of food and doing right duties. When you lose your dignity, you go astray."

I first met Shyam while I was a working mother, exhausted, agnostic, and depleted, with two babies in diapers. His psychological and physiological cures bridged the Western and Eastern traditions with equal and sensible ease, whilst I floundered between. His restoration of my sanity and health is a similar story shared by many grateful recipients.

This book is divided into several sections, initially constellated around the many pictures located in our archives and shared at his memorial. This idea I must credit to Dr. Sandra Canzone, whom Shyam named the "healing angel of Santa Fe." The pictures began to form a pattern of themes, followed by the amazing quotations and texts found in my transcribed notes of his talks, videos, and audios accumulated in his patient teachings over thirty-three years. All his words constitute the content. I have given his special quotes in italics on the chapter pages to allow these gems to stand out. Some sections include essays or extractions from Wisdom Wave (the nonprofit foundation centered on Dr. Shyam's teachings through his talks, writings, newsletters, videos, and audios). Other sections simply include a series of quotes that are loosely related to a topic. Very often the collection of quotes on a theme encompasses a wide range of years. I hope the reader will find such collections to be provocative for self-inquiry, which often was his intention. Even contemplating one or two of the paragraphs will reap a treasure trove of insights and even a profound revolution of the personality.

The book formed itself in an initial organic fashion that turned into chapters:

Chapter I: Messages he repeated over time

Chapter II: Origins in India with beloved friends

Chapter III: Origins of Wisdom Wave, his foundation started in the United States

Chapter IV: Vast Origins of Creation, with philosophical thoughts on origins of the universe

Chapter V: Fostering the Human Constitution with Ayurvedic teachings

Chapter VI: Sthitaprajna - To be Established in the Self emphasized his love of and stress upon the Vedic concept of self-dignity and firmness in upholding the Divine Self

Chapter VII: The Basic Trinity of Conduct, emphasized by Shyam as the backbone of all life

Chapter VIII: Healing, a section that will hopefully inspire future writings on that vast subject, which he lovingly exemplified in all of his relationships with friends and patients

Chapter IX: Liberation From the Narrow Ego Towards Self-realization emphasizes the need for sanity and release from the pettiness of the narrow ego. This section culminates with the bright prospect of the human realization of the Divine Self, residing within.

Chapter X: *Summun Bonum*: The Highest Good gives a summation of his teachings through his words alone. In this first book since his death, I do not feel confident to summarize, paraphrase, or represent his words with my own. Thus, I am closing with his thoughts and words, which can only do justice to the teachings of this majestic light bringer.

One of his last messages to us was that we needed to dissect ourselves. Self-honesty and self-study were paramount among his teachings, to face ourselves exactly as we are and bring every trend of the personality to light. This requires constant watchfulness, mindfulness, dedication, and supplication, allowing the *Dharma* (universal law) to uphold us. Then, he said that we did not have the capability of dissecting ourselves. He'd always been a ferocious and unswerving surgeon of the personality.

Jak Pilozof once told me that the name *Hari* was not only a name for *Lord Krishna*, but that it also carried the meaning "to scrape." Interestingly, at that time, I found myself calling Dr. Shyam *Hari*. I realized the great compassion behind his sternness and his unfailing love for us to establish ourselves in truth. I would think, "It's a hard job, but someone's got to do it." I added to that thought, "He's the best and the only one who can." This was the moment that compassion welled up because I realized he literally was the only person I'd ever known whose love was so abundant that he insisted upon us finding and embodying the truth within ourselves.

Patricia Brown, Ph.D. (Gayatri) Santa Fe, New Mexico, March, 2017

Contents

List of Figures

Individuals are identified from upper left to lower left clockwise in photos
(Within photos from right to left except first photo or where noted)
Permissions obtained

Chapter I

MESSAGES

Oh Atman, You are the primordial atom. You have given rise to millions of atoms. They are all part of You. Oh Ancient One, You are our succor and deliverance. It was You who made the first man in Your own image, and Your image never fails. It is an image ever bright and gives light to Your creation. Your encouragement is the Source of all that is good and honest.

Oh Creator, I therefore bow to Thee forever and anon. The equation You have taught to the beginning of creation is what You cherish and take delight in its ramifications. Oh, One without a second, make us Your sparks and allow us to accomplish Your original desire: that all is One and One is all! Life is a lovelier form of delight, and light is its goal.

The meaning of Avatar (Jesus Christ, Krishna, and Buddha) is that one who descends for the benefit of those who have no support. Jesus was a hook. He let himself be lifted by the Divine. It will lift you up, and you will not come down dharmically in truth or consequences.

Messages to Friends:

The 9 "R's":
Relent, Relax, Reflect, Reassess, Remember, Rejuvenate, Reassure, Reconstruct, Rejoice!

Awareness; Freedom; Letting go of the past; Fearlessness; Love of heart;
Compassion of mind; Forgiveness; Charity (give and take); Tolerance; Peace:
Human Community; Authenticity or Utter Truth to Oneself; Honesty
We have kept ourselves on an even keel without inferiority or superiority complexes.
You have become bold enough without cowardice.

The Choice Is Life

Generally, people only connect to body, mind, and spirit as an inept presence in their lives. There is no sense of meaning or realization of function or purpose, other than a primitive orientation to the acquisition of conditioned desire. Even modern thinkers and writers never quite define body, mind, and spirit, although making numerous and constant reference to these terms. A search for their underlying connection and meaning in life involves the comprehension of body, mind, and spirit in the context of their potential field of activity and the conduct of the life process. To discern these three components present in every living being is to see the immanent factors that contribute to body, mind, and spirit. They are functional properties of a continuous process originating from time immemorial. To see this is to realize their hidden meaning and to canonize them. The Spirit is the first born, the mind is the second, and the body is the result of their connection. The body has a comparatively more temporary existence than the mind. The mind and Spirit express through the body. In the spiritual sphere, realization is important. The ego does not want to belong to God but only to itself. To understand how the presence of body, mind, and spirit are conducive to the performance and projections in the comportment of life requires meditation upon function and meaning. To examine your life is meditation. Not to compromise with your examination brings an attitude, which increases the potential of the spirit to yield a genuine insight into the body and the mind. The meaning of their presence comes to light, bringing penetration into the ways of dexterity in the world to work toward a peaceful and profitable solution. The individual body merges into the universal body and flows in life as mind and spirit. Mind, then, becomes a constant and helpful companion in the process of living a life.

Reaching this point means that the choice is life, and the will is redeemed from dormant to active. Here is the sanctum sanctorum of balance and harmony. Our life is a rendition, not perdition. It is a thunder and not a plunder! The majesty of life is the tapestry of living, inspired by He to whom the heart belongs, who's always in my heart.

Without cherishing life, there is no pursuit of yoga or the union of body, mind, and spirit. Without their peaceful union, there is no accumulation of merit. Without merit or worthiness, the Spirit does not bestow pure insight. Without insight, the understanding of the gambit of dexterity in approaching the world is absent. Without cherishing life and merit, life itself is not lived, but is consigned to mediocrity and ineptitude.

Faith: The Real Choice

When we separate creation from the Creator, we build up a different world, create a different world. And then it creates suffering. Somebody got married. I told her, "It may not be a good thing for you now… think about it. You are creating misery for yourself." [She responded,] "No! I want to do it now!" therefore she did. Now she is crying. So she created. We create all this and say 'I'm suffering.' So, when you have that faith, you'll not suffer. I don't think anybody has bad intentions… nobody wants to become sick, nobody wants to suffer. Nobody wants to. But, you still suffer. If you have a choice, you will not make a choice to suffer. No, we don't have choice.

The real choice is faith. If that is there, everything is hunky dory!

In one stretch of illumination you reach a point, when you are at a crossroads, between the higher and the lower. You are confronted by the Truth, and that reveals the meaning of faith. You are confronted by the Truth. That's what stops you, in your tracks… the Truth. If you are going straight on the road, the path, and the powerful Illumination comes from there… that's the first morning of your life. Faith is the dynamic action of reality, with reality, into reality, beyond reality. Faith is one step beyond God. That is one of the greatest Vedic sayings.

We don't know God at all, in a sense; still, we say we have faith in God. Faith in a very powerful person is not really faith; it is fear. God is all powerful. There is no power beyond that, as far as we can imagine. We have been told by scriptures and great pundits and philosophers, there is no greater power than God, Who is the most powerful, all powerful. And we have faith in that all powerful because that power doesn't frighten us. We have no fear in that power. Even with *gurus,* faith comes out of fear. Even in what you call Masters, the faith comes out of fear.

There was a communist professor whom I knew very well. He took off his shoes as he came near a temple, and made a gesture of *pranams.* Somebody asked him immediately, "Communists don't believe in God; why are you prostrating?" He said, "I know, I don't believe, but I do it, in case there is God!" That's the fear. We do many things out of fear… but in the Almighty God, there is no fear. Therefore, you have got faith. We don't even question that faith. And what is this faith actually? When there is no fear, we have God in Love. God is nothing but Love, so we have got faith in that aspect of God, which is Love, which is all powerful, which is beneficial. When we are in difficulties, we pray, so that God may help us in some way.

Faith is the dynamic action of reality, That which you are. Beyond this God or what you call The Creator, is nothing but creative energy, that dynamic creative energy in which we participate. We vigilantly and strongly and powerfully participate in that principal of creation. That's faith. Faith is energy. Faith is the kernel of religion. Faith is the inspirational energy behind religion and spirituality. So therefore it becomes a dynamic action of reality, in the absolute sense. That's faith; the dynamic action is the awareness, also creation. Awareness is nothing but energy.

But we can say, "I've got faith in this, faith in that," and all those things. We can fake all the faiths. Whatever we think we know is the illusion of reality. And, if you truly know reality, you are not different from That. See, you cannot separate yourself from that force, so that's One-ness. Then faith is yourself. But, we cannot fake the faith that is faithfulness. Faith is faithful to the lover of faith.

In time, what happens is you come into that reality that is yourself, not something different. You come to the Abyss, and then fear comes, terrible fear comes, and you come back. You want to get away from it. That's where God dwells. There's the Abode of God, the Abyss. Void, Total Silence. Yet it is still dynamic. That is called still-point of silence and that is one of the aspects of the Divine birth. That's the womb of God, the void, the womb where everything is born. Continuous birth takes place, continuously and that's when you establish in the temple or the church what we call the 'Sanctum Sanctorum," the inner sanctum. In Sanskrit there is one word, womb. When you invoke that womb, every time you worship, the Divine is born and born and born. So you are the Creator of God. You must know that. You're the Creator of God. God is your Creator. You are the Creator of God also. That's creation. It's not co-creation, which sounds like co-conspirators! It is creation. Therefore, in the end, what happens is that there is no difference between the Creator and the Created. They're all One.

Shyam
tirelessly
teaching,
supporting;
playfully and
delightfully a
fully born
human being.

Figure 2

5

On Faith

"Where there is hatred, let me sow love," said St. Francis of Assisi some 900 years ago. His prayer is used all over the world for healing, for peace, and for enlightenment. From time immemorial, human beings have used several words to achieve salvation. Even in the age of machines and science, we are accustomed to pause and ponder over certain words of positive meaning and application such as love, faith, peace, honor, harmony, and prayer. Out of all these words, I think the word "faith" is of paramount importance. The entire creation, I think, is faith inspired. Everything useful, helpful, and righteously powerful is delineated by faith.

Where there is faith, there is love;
Where there is love, there is harmony;
Where there is harmony, there is peace;
Where there is peace, there is happiness;
Where there is happiness, there is joy;
Where there is joy, there is creation.

Every created "thing" and the uncreated "no-thing" stem from faith. It is a wonderful experience to realize that faith is one step beyond God. It is, therefore, God's inspiration. The Divine vision is the vision of faith. If you take one step in the right direction in faith, all our steps and leaps in life will be of faith. There is no prejudice in faith. Love comes from faith. If God is love, then faith is God. Naturally, faith is the dynamic action of benevolence in reality. Only with faith, prayer becomes effective. It can heal, and it can make one whole.

Where there is faith, there is the rainbow of life touching all the ends
And beginnings in the eternal dimensions.
Where there is faith, there is energy of fulfillment.
Where there is faith, there is prayer, its chosen medium.
Life exists because of faith, and prayer prospers because of faith.

In the created world, prayer becomes the worthy medium or channel of faith, which transforms the cry of the human soul into Divine music set to the tune of the rhythmic creation.

If you have faith, you have love;
If you have love, you have peace;
If you have peace, you have plenty;
If you have plenty, you have joy;
If you have joy, you have health;
If you have health, you have happiness;
If you have happiness, you have the supreme ability
And insight to delight eternally with each and every Divine mystery.
Blessed are those who have faith and are not separate from faith.

May your faith prevail in the strife-ridden world and bring understanding, peace, and prosperity to those who are not intoxicated with the power of the ego and those who are faithful to their own words and promises.

May faith itself bless you with faith, the eternal inspiration of God the Creator.

Shrikrishna Kashyap (Dr. Shyam) *Satsang* Talk, 2000,
Transcribed by Zuleikha

Dear friends, good morning.

Believe in me
Have faith in God
Have faith in yourself—
If not, you fake everything!

Your mind is meticulously yours. When it is kept in a framework of life's propensities and firmness of motivation, your intelligence and interacting ability with the universe and the created world sometimes brings about conflict. The conflicts sometimes act as a stimulus for they have the energy to stimulate and ameliorate. The Creator must have a purpose in introducing conflict into the smooth waters of life so as to produce ripples, which are beautiful and enabling to purposeful action in life. When the waters become murky and the ripples are not seen as such in the context of complements and implements, the result is resentment and also empowerment. It is just like locks of hair, which beautifully blend in the wind and the breezes and the absence of both. You have a purpose in life, and that purpose is to attain the Divine grace in all your undertakings and works you do predominately in the field of selfless service to your community and contemporary amicability. The Creator is wrought with miracles and a marvelous hide and-seek game that generally helps to improve the stability of life's undertaking. My love is eternal because it is contained in a state of bliss. If you understand this much, I'll tell you more.

Love, Shyam

Here you can romance with life and
Dance with God without strife.
Sky above and land below,
Make your home under no dome
You will bless and
Bloom and work the loom.

Forces of Attraction and Repulsion

The forces of attraction and repulsion are inherent in nature as primordial principles in material creation. These forces unite and operate as unconditional love on a cosmic level. In the world, they are forces of reaction and retroaction. In the human mind, they operate as forces of love and hatred. The entire thought process is governed by the divisive influence of these forces. They are beneficial if they are understood in the light of reason and virtue. They help to discriminate right from wrong. They manage to keep the universal laws operating without disruption among the heavenly bodies and their relationships. This means that even the planets have attraction and repulsion. They stand at a particular distance. These principles promote awareness, interconnectedness, and harmony.

When thoughts become corrupted, actions become corrupted. Good and evil exist in thought and not in reality. As long as our actions are dictated by a negative thought process, we are bound to have wars, destructions, and calamities. The moment we understand the mechanism of thought, we transcend it. If we are honest to ourselves, then we transform the entire process into benevolent processes. Thoughts are sounds we hear inwardly. If we think, "Jesus," we hear "Jesus." If we think "flower," we think "flower." Since God is a good thought, every religion in the world tells us to think of God. If we do not think a good thought, we fall into a negative and discordant sound pattern. We should not, therefore, allow our minds to chatter. We still the mind by the practice of meditation and by being totally attentive to life. Thought has substance. Please do not abuse the substance! Transform it, and use it as an end to all means that cause greed and destruction.

If these laws are not understood, they have a devastating effect upon the vital functions of life. They may lead to violence, jealousy, hatred, tyranny, ingenious manipulations, and exploitations. Enslaved by ignorance, the human mind may become a playground for good and evil. It becomes possessive and envious. So, many evil thoughts enter into the field of perceptions, such as "you and I, mine and yours, my religion is better than your religion, my country is better than your country," and so on. If you observe the world, you will notice that these things are going on in every nation. There is turmoil in the world because of the lack of understanding of the human qualities as inherent in the primordial principles. If the human being can understand and go beyond all these conditions, however tempting they appear to be, the person can go beyond this vicious thought process. When the forces of attraction and repulsion are unified, they operate as serenity – just serenity.

1990

*(Editor's Note: some of these paragraphs appear in the section **"On Healing"** but are left here as part of a shorter essay)*

Messages on Himself

*Let my words filter into your mind and blow it out. My understanding is
the result of talented observation. My discourse is another course.*

In God's kingdom, I went through the unlatched back door.

*The world is on the verge of foreclosure.
I unfortunately know the inner volume of the universal catastrophe.*

I reach, not preach.

Thought is faster than light, and I am faster than that. I only think after the thoughts are over!

*My birth was at the threshold of death and my death is at the threshold
of birth. Birth and death are at the threshold of each other.*

*I wish for you to have that power. The avatars had that power but we do
not take their names sincerely. We do not follow their teachings.
Hell is full of those who do not follow the teaching.*

*My love is vast. It is a spontaneous outburst. Love is a dynamic approach to spread and propagate. You
all are doing that. The Rishis (universal sages) were transcendental. Innocence is the voice of the sages.*

*I thought I was standing alone on the orb of time. Then a host of good people were there.
You were there. All are born in the glory of God. You are the essence of the
power behind that. In one ecstatic moment, you experience your Self.*

The man who is absent is also present. In a practical sense, he is not here but he is here.

*The world is not a conducive world. One day I hope you will see a conducive world.
I will bless you all from heaven. It will take time.*

*Do not ask me what I write
Do not ask me what I sing
My songs are with the One who loves me eternally.
My writings are with Him who takes pleasure eternally.
My book of life I have kept open.
He looks upon it with open eyes and sheds light eternally.
He never closes His eyes and mingling
And I never stop writing or singing.*

*The inner sanctum of my heart has a brilliant light. It doesn't shine in the morning
or in the night. It shines in the beyond far from the human plight.*

Precepts

I.   The Word of God is God. It flows out but remains within. It gives birth to creation, which is also a blessing in all aspects. We are therefore blessed.

II.   We have received the blessing of God, and in turn we have to bless the noble and good creation. A human being is a blessing destined to bless others in a conscious way by way of creativity and compassion, which renders all things equal at the level of being.

III.   God is not a person but an omnipresent "is-ness" with order and glory.

IV.   God is a realized experience.

V.   The cosmos is a celebration of all beings in God's blessing-filled cosmos. We are fully immersed in the universe, which is in us and outside of us.

VI.   Let go and let creation be the holy blessing that it is. What prevents us from this ground? Our tendency is to grab, to control, to dictate, to possess and to cling. By letting go of this clinging to things we learn what true reverence is and what true appreciation can be. When we let go of fear, we can sink into the blessing and grace of all creation and into its Creator and more deeply into the God beyond the Creator who is the Godhead.

VII.   At every step, if we are aware, we are inspired by the mysteries of God and His creation. Be inspired by the mysteries of God and His creation. There are some mysteries that are beyond the cultural images we spin out, which only faith and revelation can reveal. This needs a breakthrough in our consciousness, a resurrection, a new birth, an awakening to a deeper truth. One such truth is that we are sons and daughters of God; therefore, we have Divine blood circulating in us. If we let go of pettiness and limiting perspectives, we can let this truth wash over us and, like God, we can create and be compassionate.

VIII. Spirituality is a growth process: the constant expansion and recreation of God's creative power and enhancement of all the potentials we have been endowed with. There is no limit to our divinity because there is no limit to divinity. It is not a matter of climbing Jacob's ladder in a competitive or compulsive way, but a spiral-like ever-expanding response that touches the limits of the cosmos and returns with real experience to our primal origin restored and reformed.

IX.   Creativity is the work of God in us. Creative works are our works as the work of God. Trinity gives birth. The trinity is being, knowing, and doing. Just being is becoming nothing. Just knowing is rationalism. Doing alone is activism. But knowing and doing that are born from being is the Divine work. We have the ability to unfold the creation by enfolding God's Word. Beauty and blessing are shared.

X.   Compassion is full spiritual maturity. To touch our own roots we must make contact with compassion and justice, mystically and prophetically. All things are born in compassion and want to return there.

XI.   Everyone is a royal person, noble and dignified, responsible for creating compassion and justice. All persons are called to such nobility.

XII.   Jesus Christ is a reminder to every one of us of what it means to be God's child. Such a birth is possible for every one of us. Put Jesus on the altar to stop altercations! He is the Word of God calling us to be the Words of God. He is the Son of God calling us to be children of God.

Spirituality

The human being is potentially Divine, essentially human, substantially natural, and intrinsically spiritual.

Spirituality is not a high intellectuality, not idealism, not an ethical turn of mind or moral purity and austerity, not religiosity or an ardent and exalted emotional fervor, not even a compound of all these excellent things: a mental belief, creed or faith, an emotional aspiration, a regulation of conduct according to a religious or ethical formula … these are not spiritual achievements and experience. An ideal is a fad of the mind, a figment of the imagination.

Spirituality is, in its essence, an awakening to the inner reality of our being to a spiritual, self, a soul that is other than our mind, life, and body, an inner aspiration to know, to feel, to be That, to enter into contact with the greater reality beyond and pervading the universe, which inhabits also our own being.

The height of spirituality is being so transparent that you and God become One. You pass through God and God passes through you.

Laughter, newness, and joy: God is the eternally new, eternally young. To receive the Spirit of God sent when Jesus left the earth is to open ourselves up to the gifts of newness and youthfulness. Let joy be: the joy of God that creates the universe continually and calls it back to its joyful, ever new origin. Compassion also constitutes our first and primary origin. All things are born in compassion and proceed from compassion. Joy is an integral part of spiritual experience. We have to penetrate pleasure as joy to find God there, and we are to struggle and to share it. Laughter and joy are the music of the cosmos as birth takes place constantly in the Divine.

Chapter II

ORIGINS IN INDIA

Through joy and sorrow, pain and pleasure,
the soul comes to knowledge of itself.

To have real knowledge, one does not have ego. It is not the "I," just existence.

You have to exert your soul power and be an author of your life.

Two impediments to self-knowing are lacking and leaking!

You cannot know God,
You only can love God…

If a man does not find the temple in his heart,
he will never find his heart in the temple.

ORIGINS
Migration from Indian roots

Figure 3

Beloveds in India

*If the body becomes the mind of the
Spirit, and the Spirit becomes the
body of the mind,
there is integration.*

Figure 4

15

Meditation is to know the meditator when the meditator is absent. When there is only meditation, not a single thought in the mind, that mind is energy. Meditation expands our consciousness and encompasses the whole creation.

Meditation is not to go out, but to go in. It is to know one's self in every aspect of what I am, in every relationship; in connection with my relationship with the world, with people, to animals, plants, trees, the sky, the sun, the moon, to the galaxies, to the whole of creation - to know myself as all those things, not just one thing, not just a petty myself, my ego.

Human beings should be aware of every action, totally aware. Watch the mind. Mind that watches the mind. If mind is confused, the confused mind watches. In modern times, when you sit for meditation, you get caught in the methodology of it. When you sit, the mind still chatters. This is not meditation. People say "I can't stop the mind." If you are always aware, giving total attention to whatever you do, then what does the mind do? It is attending totally. If the mind merges with the heart, then you encompass the whole world. You need not be a master of yourself, but don't be a slave of yourself. Be what you are.

Figure 5

16

Simple Guidelines

Friends, hear me in awareness.

What I have to say in fairness.

We can exchange words and ideas.

We can exchange thoughts and good will.

We can exchange harmony and fun.

We can exchange works and joys.

We can exchange smiles and laughs.

We need not exchange opposites of all.

If the mind is in the right direction.
There is no need for strife and struggle.

If the heart is properly provided,
There is no need for sorrow and suffering.

If the person is well guided,
There is no need for hatred and jealousy.

If the constitution is divinely grounded,
There is no need for anger and prophecy.

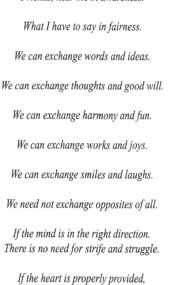

Hari's Name

Keep your heart open,
Sanctify with devotion.
You will be free from perversion.

Take the name of Shri Hari
You will have no worries.

Make your day a poem,
Without the usual mayhem.
Enjoy the happiness
*   that may come.*

Take the name of Shri Hari
You will have no worries.

May you have wonderful days.
Walk with pride the righteous ways.
May you have bliss always.

Take the name of Shri Hari
You will have no worries.

Figure 6

Figure 6

Chapter III

ORIGINS OF WISDOM WAVE

Brahman (God) is the only real entity.

Order is, essentiality, spirituality in action.

Discipline is, delightfully, mind in harmony.

ORIGINS of Wisdom Wave

Figure 7

Letters Written at the Inception of Wisdom Wave - 1990

Dear Friends, Salutations;

I am thankful to you for making the emergence of Wisdom Wave a reality. At the very outset, I would like to point out that Wisdom Wave is not a sect, cult, creed of some kind of organized religion fermenting and flustering around names, forms, and personalities. It is a way of life leading to the gate of light, radiating the sovereign principle of truth in its chaste and unbiased movement. It is not an abstraction but an absolution from addiction, deception, dereliction, and corruption. In short, it is a psychological and spiritual afflatus for material well-being, and a faith of many faces expressing the struggle, the strife, the triumph, and the graceful surrender and searching for many more in the waves of sorrow and the ripples of joy. It is also a way to relate, to relive, and to rejoice.

It is encouraging to note that the founding fathers and mothers of Wisdom Wave are already collecting useful information to ascertain whether there exists a feasible environment for opening a temple of wisdom to promote health, wholeness, and right understanding. This will enable anyone needing help to meet life in harmony, peace, and progress.

What is essentially needed is your wholehearted support. Support as you all know, is strength, and strength is the key to success.

In fine, I do beseech you to be free to enroll as [a] member of Wisdom Wave with your contributions. Your might and magnanimity are bound to make this foundation the unshaking and unfaltering voice of dignity for the conscience of mankind.

Love, Light, Peace,

Shyam
(S. Kashyap)

Communication, Consultation, Cooperation, Compliance

Communication, consultation, cooperation, and compliance are the basic requirements for any organization evolving in the orbital space of human aspiration and spiritual sempiternity. Order and discipline are of paramount importance for the process of growth and dignity. Order is, essentially, spirituality in action; discipline is, delightfully, mind in harmony. To realize this simple truth is to live life abundantly and gracefully in loving action.
Shyam

Dr. Shyam shared this with everyone
who visited him in Santa Fe:
The light of God ever shines.
The love of God ever abides.
The flower of Life never fades.
The Spirit of Man never dies.

*The Purpose of Wisdom Wave is to foster the
upliftment of humankind through universal
spiritual philosophy, without discrimination or
affiliation, teaching a way of living which can
bring order to human life with profound order,
awareness and creativity.*

Figure 8

Early Moments
in the Formation Wisdom Wave

Figure 9

23

Spirituality, Faith, and Religion

Spirituality, faith, and religion are all wonderful words if you know the meaning of them. But we generally don't. Religion is the last of the triangle. Our spirituality reflects into our ego, and then that kind of "spirituality" has the quality of the ego. Unfortunately, we tend to create the idea in the ego, and we call it spirituality. When this idea from the ego is extended into belief, it becomes delusion. Then we talk about religion, and that becomes conflict. In this confusion, we always work in ignorance, in darkness, and therefore the whole thing becomes a mess. So, we created a great mess in the world. In order to recover ourselves from this mess, we use all these methods and prayers, but we do them without faith, without religiousness. I don't mean a specific religion like Christianity or Buddhism. Religiousness is the triumph of the innocent mind, the triumph of the innocent mind in the everyday life. The meaning of an innocent mind is a mind that is not conditioned by anything. It is innocent, pure, very clear, has all clarity in it. It is not conditioned by anything, it doesn't hold onto content, so therefore it is not conditioned by anything. Therefore, this mind has access to the universality of the spirit. Universality is spirituality and faith. Religion, if you take the root word, means binding back to one's faith, that there is something higher than myself, that there is something called spirit, which is in me and everything else, so I don't have a difference with anyone else. That is the language of the spirit, that's what faith means, that's what religion means, a faith binding-back, binding back to our source, to our core. And where is that? It is in our own heart. So our heart has a silent space, where it doesn't thump. It is very scientific, I tell you that. There is one place in the heart that doesn't thump, which has nothing to do with the arteries or the structure and function of the body. This place in the heart is very expansive and very silent. That is what we mean by silence in the mind, or stilling the brain. The brain should be still in order to silence the mind because if the brain is still, the mind is silent. It's a chemical process that goes on, in this two and a half pound brain, which is like a jellyfish in a way. This brain creates all the problems, and that is connected to the ego. The brain actually is not connected to the mind, and it is not connected to any genuine spiritual thought. So when we do not function with spirituality, faith becomes a delusion, and religion becomes just a conflict. That is happening in the world, you see.

Spirituality and faith and religion are a triangle. At the top of the triangle is spirituality, and what is spirituality actually? It is nothing but abiding in the spirit, in truth, in faith, and in reality. But what happens is, in the course of our life on this earth... we try to interact with people [and] we encounter a lot of people who talk about faith and religion and spirituality. We want to know what spirituality is. We want to be spiritual. Everybody is yearning for that spirituality; something called spirituality. So we have a lot of methods like yoga, prayer, and meditation. Yoga is a simple sophisticated approach to the mental horizon. Yoga is to join the self to the Divine Self or to yoga principles. But it has been misinterpreted and we think we're "doing good."

Meditation is mediation between you and your God. In meditation, what we do is try to understand ourselves. It's not a going-out but a going-in. Meditation is trying to know one's self in every aspect, in every relationship, in connection with the world, with people, with animals, with the whole creation; the plants and trees, the sky the sun, the moon, the planets, and all the galaxies. These are so expansive. So meditation is to know myself as all that. Not just a petty "myself," my ego, but as an expansion. Meditation expands our consciousness to all these things and encompasses the whole creation, all the universes and all the galaxies and all the planets. We become a planetarium.

Consciousness is a beautiful movement, an ecstatic life system. In one moment of the fullness of experience, you are not there. It gives you complete freedom. It cannot be manipulated. One experience of bliss is worth a thousand blinks!

But generally, what happens is that in our ego-centeredness, we always say we are separate from each other, we are different. One belongs to Christianity, one belongs to Hinduism, one belongs to Buddhism, or one belongs to Islam. We created these groupings to separate ourselves from each other.

In our effort to face the situation, we meet in *satsang*, in a gathering of "truth seekers." We try to understand each other in the higher sense, from the sense of spirituality, from universality. We try to work the faith and religion through this spirituality, and then religion and faith have a meaning, otherwise not. Then there is oneness; we see everything in universality that is equanimity. We see everything as equal, not something different from ourselves. If you have a fence around your house, anyone who is outside the fence is the other; if there is no fence he is not the other, he is one of you. So the idea of "other" has really created the problem of "otherness." Then you think of the other world, the world, which is antagonistic to us, which doesn't belong to us. We always think of another world as some kind of an alien. We always have fear of the other. Because if someone comes near that side of the fence, you tell your dog that somebody is there, and the dog will go and bark because the other is not yourself. So this is illogical, in a sense, and irrational. We think it is very rational to think of the other world because we do not know this world itself. Therefore we think of another world that doesn't exist as a separate world. And we can give any name to it; that is a label. We fight for the labels. The whole world is fighting for labels.

Transformation should take place on an individual basis, not with external parameters. Every individual is unique, with his or her own scent and taste. Like a prime number, an individual cannot be divided. For the last three thousand years in recorded history, people talked about peace, harmony, so many methods that are just words. No real peace. So many are crucified, slaughtered, in the name of religion. God-Transformation should come on an individual basis. Every individual becomes part of the entire society, just like a bouquet of flowers: Different flowers are there and should be in the bouquet.

The "Be-er" and the "Doer"

Something seems to confuse us many times. In Christianity, we hear mostly about the personal God, while in Eastern teachings the focus is mostly on the impersonal. This seemingly opposite viewpoint causes some to think there are two different "gods." We can ask how do they relate to each other or are they merely concepts?

From my understanding, the personal and the impersonal are not two different gods nor are they concepts. They are two sides of the same coin. The nameless Truth has manifested itself as the entire universe, so every form you see, hear, touch, taste, smell, and think about is God. God's cosmic body is the totality of all bodies within it; God's mind is the sum total of all minds. Just as each of you have billions of "cells" in your body, so it is that each of your body-mind complexes is only one of the billions of "cells" in the personal or dynamic aspect of God. He or She, whichever word you choose to mean God, moves, thinks animates, creates, sustains, and dissolves universes. This personal aspect is God's expression, power, or energy. So we have these two aspects of the Divine, just as it tells us in Genesis: the Mother (the personal) and the Father (the impersonal). Now the Mother or personal principle is the entire universe—all of its forms, as all form, is the Mother. We are all part of the Mother. The Mother has many faces. Some are wrathful, some are tender. The Mother covers the world. We cover the world with the Mother through our daily life situations. Our bodies are part of the Mother. We feed on the Mother (the earth). We absorb the Mother (air, light, water, food). We literally feed at the Mother's breast continuously. She is the life, the vibration, the energy of the Universe. We keep growing inside as we feed more and more. We literally have to consume the Mother, the beauty and the violence. Taking all that energy, use it in order to stay with God.

In contrast to all this dynamism of the personal aspect, the impersonal is pure awareness; and that is still and silent. The Psalmist says, "Be still and know that I am God." This is the Reality, the ground and substratum of our being. It is existence, consciousness, and bliss. It is the all-pervading light, pathless, changeless, nameless, formless, and indivisible. This is the Father, the *Brahman*, meaning the "all" or "infinite." It is like the number one before a long string of zeros. Take away the one, and the zeros come to nothing. So we see when all forms subside, only the impersonal reality remains.

As to the relationship between the personal and the impersonal, think of a statue and a block of stone. The statue is personal and the block of stone is impersonal. Stone is the stuff that constitutes the statue. Or think of a gold earring. The earring, a function, is personal. The gold, the stuff of which the earring is made, is impersonal. We can state this another way. The impersonal is the "Be-er;" the personal is the "Doer." And where do we come in? We are "It." With our memories, desires, likes and dislikes, our talents, personality, body, and mind, we are a microcosmic unit in a macrocosmic body of the personal (the Mother). Our real identity is impersonal awareness, pure being - consciousness - bliss. As pure being, we are unattached, cosmic, silent, and eternal. No calamity, torture, or anything we do or think can affect that.

Now you can ask: If my mind-body complex is a part of the personal aspect of God and if my awareness is also cosmic, then what is left? Who or what is "I?" This is the great cosmic joke, the great illusion, the myth, called in the East, *Maya*, because there isn't any separate "I." To realize this is the reason we seek, read, meditate, and the reason that we take birth in a form time after time, into form after form. We are like a cup filled with ocean water that floats on the surface of the ocean. The cup thinks that it is totally individual, an island unto itself. This thought itself creates the contours of the cup. The more entrenched the "I" thought becomes, the denser and more impermeable are its contours.

Now, how do we get out of this bind? Spiritual practices will thin out the "I." Practice makes the cup porous. One day the cup becomes so porous that it dissolves, and the water within merges with the water without. Really, there was never any difference between them, but when that knowledge becomes experience, and then the wheel of birth and death comes to a halt. So then at long last we have come home.

Wisdom Wave asserts and affirms:
The right and responsibility of the individual's search for the truth within
That truth abides above and beyond the limits of intellectual conceptualization
or dogmatic doctrine
The existence of one conscious, immanent and transcendent Spirit
The freedom and the responsibility of the individual
The abstention from submitting to another person's spiritual authority
The possibility of dignity, wisdom, creativity and awareness in the
growth and fulfillment of the individiual
The need for service to others as a vehicle to encourage freedom of inquiry,
humanitarian assistance and the profound application of spiritual principles

Figure 10

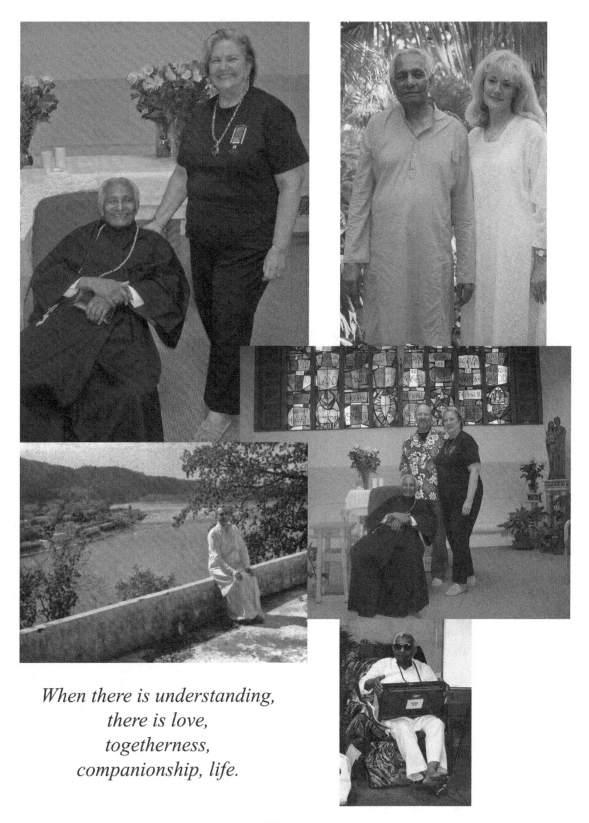

When there is understanding,
there is love,
togetherness,
companionship, life.

Figure 11

Chapter IV

VAST ORIGINS OF CREATION

That which gives life has a right to take it away.
Annihilation keeps discipline in the world. Ten years after a fire in the forest,
growth comes with more vigor.

Yama (the god of death) keeps this discipline. Yama is the law giver.

Death is a renewal process. Birth is more difficult than death.

When you complete your life mission, you merge into God,
and God appears before the truth in you.

You do not die; only the "I" dies. The body is dispersed and the essence passes into the light and
into supreme awareness. The spark of energy goes to whatever convenient place there is.
When the "I" goes, you become immortal.

The Udhava Gita says that sound is related to darkness.
Out of the darkness pierced by sound comes Light.
It comes out of Will, not intention; therefore it has no tension.

The created world always has darkness.
Darkness contracts. Light expands.
Ignorance is equated with darkness. It only contracts.
Ignorance is that which ignores light.
Yet the underlying element is delight.

The Word of God gives birth to creation. Seed words are found in the smallest units of creation,
in the atoms, in the cells in our system and in the world. Everything has a sound.
Creation is bound by sound.
We have to bless the word of God. The Jivatma is the oversoul that blesses.

One seed sprouted and branches became the multiplicity. One atom was not manipulated.
It produced all the other atoms.

Shiva Shakti is the Totality

Shiva is pure consciousness, and *Shakti* is the power of pure consciousness. The core of *Shiva* is Light. The core of the human being is light, is Spirit. *Ma Shakti* is supreme power and must be joined to *Purusha*, the supreme human being. The core of *Shakti,* Nature, or *Prakriti,* is darkness. Without the light, power is misused. Only when power is joined to the light can real creation occur. Power, however, by its nature is corrupting. When power is associated with unbridled ego, it causes great harm. That is the force of darkness, joined both to a terrible ego and a cowardly ego. When power is joined to the Light of Spirit, it inspires to good deeds and creates a golden glow.

The all is nothing but the "I," which is present in everything.

*Meditation is to know one's self
in every aspect of what I am,
in every relationship; in connection with
the whole of creation.
Right relationship is to know
we come from the same Source.
Universal brotherhood realizes
we are from the same essence.*

Figure 12

33

Mother's Day and Creation

Something's Synergy and Something's Energy

The *Vedas*, the oldest scriptures of the world, state that Mother is dawn and father is dark. Most religions say in the beginning, there was the word. The word was God, and the word was with God. But the Eastern people have a different thing. They always ask this question: What was before the beginning? What was the beginning, and what was before the beginning? There was something. The beginning has some base, so, before that, there was something. After the beginning we have all those stories. Something was there or no-thing? No-thing was there, I can tell you that. No-thing was there, but something else was there. Surely, something else was there. In the Indian scriptures it is said *Brahman* was not, He had no form, nothing was there. We call Him *Brahman* because He's expanding; it was not even space, not even time. *Brahman* means *Brasad*, which means to expand. It went on expanding. A bubble formed, the egg of *Brahman*. This creation is *Brahmanda*, the egg of *Brahma*. He didn't know what to do, even He was not! Even He was not there.

Essentiality was there. Matter was there, materiality was there. The unreal was there, but the reality was not there. Without sound, there is sound. See how complicated it is. This Brahman, he could not resist the energy. He is no form, He…She… there was nothing there. He and She were one. The energy was one. It formed itself … it is *Svayambhu*, caused by itself. Nobody else caused it, [it was] caused by itself. *Svayambhuva* means it became Itself. You see, the Being, whatever the Being was, the Being becomes; so it is becoming Itself. Out of its own volition? Whatever It is …. We don't have words for that. Some call it *Brahmana*, whatever the entity was there at that time. It's very subtle, nobody could see, nobody could hear. Then burst open the egg. It became two. They became two. Out of that came one form, a man's form and a woman's form. The remainder of the egg split into everywhere. There was nobody to hear the sound. So why do you say Big Bang?! That was after the beginning. Not before the beginning. What happened is that the egg exploded, exploded with a big bang, a great sound, but nobody was there to hear the sound. So this was a sound proposition in philosophy! Whatever remained formed again into an egg, and through *Brahman,* that entity, was created this whole universe. The same egg became two halves. One gives energy, and one acts. So there was no activity in what was not, in the before the beginning. It was calm, peaceful, and stagnant, with no movement; therefore, there was no life. Movement is life. So then these two halves collided… That's how this whole thing began. When anti-matter and matter collide, a lot of good things are produced. Polarity produces movement.

You know what's after the beginning. One part of the egg became the female. Otherwise it would not have hatched. *Brahman* would not have hatched an egg. So the female was necessary to hatch the egg. That is called the *Adi Shakti* or the "primordial power." It's a prime ordeal. When a Mother tries to give birth to a child she has to go through an ordeal. The first ordeal that the female principle went through was to create the world, create the whole thing, nature, all the creatures, and everything. One part of *Brahman*, when that thing exploded, made the sun, moon, the stars, sky, space, then the animals. Everything else came from That.

But human beings didn't come in the beginning, but before the beginning. Humans came before the beginning… That was the *Purusha*, before the beginning. The human is a part of the Divine; you must know that. He was not in all those things. So now all over the world, especially the Western world today, is celebrated the Mother's day, whether they like the Mothers or not! So from the Prime Ordeal was a moment when life came. That moment was a movement. From that moment comes the movement. In one of the beautiful poems of Rabindranath Tagore, he extolls the Mother saying that, "Without you, I could not have been here. Without you, I'd not have been *Rabindra*." *Rabindra* means the "king of light." Without you, even Einstein said, "I would not have been a scientist." I'd not have been... all have said this, "I'd have not been without the Mother." Even the great Shankaryacharya said, "Sons can be very bad, fathers can be very bad, but not Mothers." He ascertains the Mothers cannot be bad. He became a monk and went away when he was fourteen years old. He left his Mother and went away. And then suddenly it struck him, "If my Mother dies, what will happen to me? I will be ungrateful." So he goes back. His Mother had died. He was sixteen. There were very heavy rains and thunderstorms. There was no wood, no wood to burn... In those days there was no electric crematorium. So how would they cremate with terrible rains for days and days? They said there was no dry wood, we have to wait for 15 or 20 days. He said, "I don't want to keep my Mother like that." So he carried her in his own hands and cut some banana trees. Banana trees are always very wet. Banana trees cannot be burnable wood at all. He put the banana trees down, put the body on top, and lit it with his own fire. With his own fire he lit wet banana leaves and cremated the body. Shankaryacharya had that great love for his Mother, even though he had to leave the home, because that was the bounden duty to go and do God's work. Mother and Mother Earth are greater than any heaven. To say you owe Her nothing makes you irresponsible.

The most controversial and hated figure in the Bible is God. Nobody understood anything about the Bible. The God we project as God, or the concept people have about God, didn't work because God became a concept and not reality. This caused the greatest chaos because everything we based our religions upon was just a concept. Therefore we are at loggerheads. We are born individually, independently, and we are supposed to live together, but we don't. The Mother figures, Mary Magdalene, whom they said was the whore, was a great Mother. The Mother of Shankaryacharya, and many more, are great Mothers. Because of Mary, Jesus became a recluse and faced the crucifixion. Otherwise he would have escaped. He didn't escape because of his Mother. He loved his Mother so much. When he said "Oh God, do not forsake me," he was telling that to his Mother because to him the female and male God are the same. They're not different. So he called out to the Godhead, whom he called God. So he didn't call God a loggerhead, he called Him the Godhead. And we have become at loggerheads, right?

One of the services adopted by the Roman Catholics is called "A Mass to Virgin Mary," that means[1] at that time they extolled Her as a Goddess. And they do a Mass every year, where it is clearly stated that She says, "Before the beginning, I was there when He created all those things. I was there when He created all the mountains, I was there when He created the oceans, and I was there all the

---

[1] Proverbs VIII: 22-35 in the Roman Missal for the Mass of the Immaculate Conception gives this translation of a primordial voice of the feminine: "The Lord possessed me in the beginning of His ways before He made anything, from the beginning. I was set up from eternity, and of old, before the earth was made. The depths were not as yet, and I was already conceived; neither had the fountains of waters as yet sprung out; the mountains with their huge bulk had not yet been established. Before the hills, I was brought forth. He had not yet made the earth, nor the rivers, nor the poles of the world. When He prepared the heavens, I was there. When, with certain law and compass, he enclosed the depths; when He established the sky above, and poised the fountains of water; when He composed the sea with its bounds and set a law to the waters that they should not pass their limits; when He balanced the foundations of the earth, I was with Him, forming all things and was delighted every day, playing before Him at all times, playing in the world; and my delight is to be with the children of men. He that shall find me shall find life and shall have salvation from the Lord."

time, whatever He did. Without me He could not do anything." This is the ascertainment of the female power from the beginning, before the beginning.

Before the beginning was and is the female power, with no name. We can call it the miraculous atom. Atom is *Atman*; it comes from the Sanskrit word, the Self without a self. It is the mystical atom also. It is the mysterious atom that started evolving, evolving, and evolving, a vertical not perpendicular evolvement. There were 184 axes, spinning vertically. That's how it created. Everything spun out of it. Water spun out of it, mountains spun out of it, whole earths spun out of it. With all those things that earth holds, She is considered the Supreme Mother.

In the beginning there was the word. What was before the beginning? There was only sound. What sound was there? The sound forms into a word, forms into a letter, actually: an alphabet. Letters form into a word, a word in that evolutionary process, going spinning, spinning, spinning and become a word. That's how in the Jewish tradition the first letter is *Alef*. In Arabic, it's *Aleef*, the same thing, *Aleph, Aleef*; the second word is *Beta, Bet*... Letters are alive. But the word didn't come in the beginning at all, just a letter, and that the Indians say is the OM (or *Aum*.) *Aum* is the first sound that came out of the ocean that came out of *Brahman*'s egg. So the truth is not the "Word was with God." It's not with God, the word created God. Suppose you didn't know any words, no letters, how can you create a God? How can you create anything? You are also the word because you are born in the image of God, so you are also the word. You have that importance; you are equal to God, because you are the same word. So the word was God, and the human is the word also. The word was with the human and that is also the superhuman, the superhuman person.

All Mothers are considered to be Supreme Mothers; even the sisters are Supreme Mothers, Mother Superiors, right? Prioress, Mother Superior, and so on. St. Benedict was Italian. He explained in two sentences that if the Mother would not have been, even Christianity would not have been there. Jesus Christ would not have been there. No religion would have been there. No spirituality would be there. The fundamental Spirit is the Spirit that created everything, even God. Even God. It created God. Therefore the Mother is very important.

We are so ungrateful to Motherhood. You know a man can be a father, a husband, a brother, anything. A Mother can be a wife; [she] can be a sister, a grandmother. It's an evolution, a process of evolution, so the basic principle is to honor that. And this is honored in India everywhere. They honor the Mothers. It has come from time immemorial. This Mother's day comes in the festival of lights. In those days Mothers were to be worshiped and wives were worshiped also. Wives are Mothers also. The light shines through the womb of creation. The *Brahman* came a little after that ... The egg was about to break, and He jumped into it. And it closed. So He was in the womb of creation. Then the egg broke. The Creator was in the womb of creation. The womb always belongs to the Mother, Her womb of creation. Every Mother is a womb of creation. She creates human beings. There can be civilized citizenship in an uncivilized world created by half human beings who are uncivilized. You must know that. And those few truly civilized ones are in the sense of not having ego. Pride and ego make a lot of injustice in the world. That's the cause of injustice and all the miseries we have created in the world. Ego and pride, pride and prejudice...Motherhood started before the beginning. That's how the Mother is worshiped. You surrender to the Motherhood. Even God surrendered to it. God surrendered to the Mother. He was the representative of God anyway. Jesus Christ was an incarnation. He was his Father's son, son of the Godhead; he was a god also in a sense. So he worshiped Mary for having given birth to him, not to suffer in the world but to uplift the sufferers by his own suffering.

The passion of Christ is an inbuilt passion for morality. How many of us do this in the world? We try to hold the tail of the winning horse. Even Madeline Albright, a brilliantly bright woman, said, "God is with us, are we with God?"

Mother's Day

This is the day the world honors the Mother. Mother is not different from God. Your life is Mother also. Ramakrishna fell on the feet of his wife as the Mother. Ramakrishna was great. He was married because in the Indian tradition they have arranged marriage. It was the same thing with Anandamayi Ma. Her husband fell at her feet. He became her first disciple. If you give that importance, that embellishment, that nourishment, to that idea of the Mother, you'll never be in difficulties. You'll never have conflicts; you'll never have these 783 conflicts! If you count all those conflicts per day for all the people on earth, how many billions will it be? I don't think you'll have any mathematical calculations for that. So we become a mathematical impossibility also. See but we are calculative, very calculative, but we cannot calculate this. Our own follies we cannot calculate. What kind of mathematics do you use to ascertain the integrity, the involvement, the efficiency, the motivation, the criterion of a human being to be a fully born human being? Every day is Mother's day. Every minute is a Mother's day, I tell you. It is not just once a year. Every day you must have that respect for That. Through the Mother you can be God; because He is also Mother's son. God has not come out of men. This is a penchant of God. He created women, you must respect it. Mother's duty is far superior to father's duty. Both are necessary because only the duality only creates. God is very intelligent. He made man and woman. There is a saying in India: "Where women are happy, pleased, happy, blissful, there God dwells." He wants to dance also. He wants to enjoy also. Discard the mother at your own peril. The presence of God is only there where women are honored, worshipped.

Mother's Day, May, 2006

When You were Born
1995

When You were born,
The world was sound and still
There was no gong or bell.
The night was silent.
The clouds were vibrant.
The moon played hide and seek with patience.
The stars twinkled in brilliance.
There was no north or south.
There was no east or west,
Only the middle ground where everything was at rest.

Figure 13

The Mother gives you a place in Her bosom when you die.

Father's Day

All the fathers, including the Founding Fathers of the United States, represent God the Father in everybody. A father is equated to the Heavenly Father, the "I Am," the all-pervading power of God. He within us tells us to cherish the Father and behave like God. He chastises His children as the Bible says, "Whom God loveth is chastised." The Father principle is truth as the law, and the Mother principle is truth as love. Through the purity of water, everything is conducted. Through the purity of the human heart, everything is conducted. We have to invoke this purity. Depression is a disease that is a habit. Not to go into depression is intelligent. Depression causes deprivation and troubles everyone. The answer given by the Father is to find the answers in yourself, to face the problems and triumph over them. The main point of human life is to face ourselves squarely, be exposed and succeed. It is not bad to expose our faults. We must have the spine to face ourselves. It is not to suppress these faults, which causes a crippling sensation and paralyzes the psyche. If the psyche is lost, everything is lost. If you are not careful, you can become zombies. Avoid cultivating negative qualities.

The psyche never dies, but it is also where God can have a sex change! It is the repository of mythological forces. Every story has a background. Truth is stranger than fiction. We need a very expanded view of life as a sequential experience. All experiences are important. We don't see this because we get engrossed in our own pride, prejudice, and limitations. Truth is not confined to what we think we are or should be. The series of experiences go into the formation of human life, which is always informed. Formation and information are not the same. Where the flame of truth burns in your heart is where your heart sends out truth all around. Depression is an artificial thought and wish fulfillment that makes us live in fear. Diseases have no real answers except those residing in the austere, all-pervading mind. Purity of mind is what attracts. A mind that doesn't mind itself minds everyone else. God's mind is bereft of attractions and repulsions. It is so important to have a sane mind [that] is very strict. Truth is the only ladder that lifts you up and takes you to the highest point of realization. Here there is an explosion, and a bright light spreads everywhere. Every father should be like that. The highest point of realization is to be like the Heavenly Father. Give up that ego that says, "I know better than that man. Why would I have to listen to him?" Become deaf to that ego and have depth of perception. All the great people do not say they know better than someone else. They enjoy the highest point of realization and the joy of life. No sincere philosopher goes beyond the limit of practicality. Philosophy is a practical science and impeccable inner understanding. To understand everything is to understand oneself. This is not a religion where people do bad things and then live in hope. It is so important to admit one's falsehood. Progress, like it or not, will come as a punishment or a gift if we are sincere.

People may say, "My arrogance has saved me." But it's the dignity that saves. They are not the same thing. If you have dignity, you need not be arrogant at all. You are very humble with simplicity, humility, and humbleness. Dignity maintains everything. Real dignity, not acquired dignity, is your immune system. You conduct yourself with the right behavior, eating the right type of food, and doing right duties. When you lose your dignity, you go astray.

Father's Day, June 17, 2007

Primal Approach
1996

That which cannot be seen
Can be seen if you have the eyes.
Eyes are two, but visions are many. Things can be seen
But they cannot be perceived.
The inner sense
Does not belong to the senses.
It belongs to the One
Whom you behold.
Even though visions are many
They integrate in the One,
And the One is all that we need.
Living is a prime approach
To none but the One,
If we realize in our Heart of hearts
The beam of light
Which passes through all life.
The dewdrops
Which shimmer in the field.
The ripples which shine in the water
And the waves which span the ocean
Are all waters
In whatever shape they appear.
Life in minerals, in plants, in animals
And in humans
Is but life in every sense
Coming from the One and
Taking refuge in the One as and when
The One performs, pervades, purifies, perfects and prefers.

One thing you must know: It is always there, always in you. It is there,
you are there and That is there and It is everything, everywhere.
No where It is not there! But we are not everywhere. We are everywhere through that
but we are no where as a matter of fact. Wind is everywhere, in the desert,
in the African forest. Everywhere the wind is there.
These are the five elements that God created. Can you even create one element?
You came from the womb of your mother, but where were you before you were born?
You are something. You are nothing. In the nothingness, there is something.
In the Buddhist case, "sunyata" means void. In the void, there is something.
Space is there in the void. Nothing means nothing, otherwise it cannot be a void.
You cannot avoid these things!

Don't think the void is devoid of everything.
In the void there is something.
In it are the stars, moon, and sun, all those things.
You cannot devoid the void of all those things.

Figure 14

*God is nothing but a magnificent expression
of ourselves in all dimensions.*

*How do you raise the consciousness of a person?
In every person, there is a part which is totally light and
another which is partially dark,
a part which is divine and a part which is human. They
have a correlation in the core of a being,
the exact center of a being,
which is a center of the universe also.
A human being is a being beyond simply the human,
therefore the human is a being in God,
in the divine, in the universal consciousness,
which supersedes everything,
which transforms the human consciousness
which is just a part of universal consciousness.
Change is generally thought of as a substitution,
substituting coffee for tea, or tea for coffee.
Transformation is not change.*

*When you understand
your weakness,
you become strong.*

Figure 15

43

Friends
who are
part of
Shyam's
Universal
Family

Figure 16

Chapter V

FOSTERING THE HUMAN CONSTITUTION

*The Word of God gives birth to creation. Seed words are found in the smallest units of creation,
in the atoms, in the cells in our system, and in the world. Everything has a sound.
Creation is bound by sound.
We have to bless the Word of God. The* Jivatma *is the oversoul that blesses.*

The human race comes in the great wake of the Divine.

The Divine purpose is bliss. The root of knowledge is bliss.

When the mind is full of Divine Grace, nothing else will enter.

*The enrichment of the psyche is a promise of insight made to the human race
in the beginning of creation by the Great Lord.*

*Life is derived from the essence of creative forces, which in turn emanate
from the beatitude of grace and the substance of deliverance.*

An incarnation is a spark with the inkling of life process that all beings have.

The gist of life is right knowledge. The zest of life is to go on doing good.

The only way to go beyond good and evil is to go on doing good.

*God is very expensive. All the wealth in the world will not get God.
Only concentrated devotion will. Awareness is not sharpness or dullness. It is absorption.*

Love is unselfish. It is not unconditional. There is no such thing as unconditional love.

Love is the thing that makes a person to bend and kiss the ground.

We are very far away from nature and very near anarchy.

People do not want to harmonize with nature but rather with noise and conflict. You can find the harmony in conflict. Everything has its own beauty. It is better to harmonize with life.

Before you become old, become good. You cannot hurry God, nature, or old people.

Stages in Life

There is a formative stage and then a reformative stage. Preparing the ground requires a lot of things. Parents must be strict and teach children to mend their ways. Instead parents tend to accept defeat for their own fault. Lead a child onto the right path, not shielding them from the truth and reality. This makes the child worthy. Failure comes because children are shielded from truth and reality.

In the rash of youth a lot of mistakes can be done. Youth get caught up in illusion, fantasy and fallacy. To have an attitude creates a latitudinal downfall.

All things are within you. Individuation embraces the mainstream and tries to work its way through it. Finally an affirmative stage may come when we are ninety years old! Then you are affirmed to faith, truth, and order, which is confirmative. Then only do you say "I Know." When you say you are right, there is a gut feeling with the three chakras in the gut, a real feeling, not a feeling associated with outgoing habits and conditioned appealing attractions.

You are the inner human being with evolution refining the defects and corruptions of the *koshas* (sheaths of gradually subtler matter). Corruption starts from what idea you have. Corruption is a deception, leading to obsession and suppression and oppression of sequential emancipation.

Pure thought is a purgative. An honorable life knows that only God is. Your life is always a bud. It always has a chance to bloom. See that it blooms. Faith evolves the consciousness and dissolves the ego. Then all revolves around one thing, the truth, culminating in a grand finale of grace, gratitude, and love. For every opportunity, be grateful. Gratitude is happiness.

Literal love is different from eternal love. Since life is eternal, life is love. Live life adequately. Take steps one by one in life until you reach the point of emancipation. Dissolution evolves inside as taste. *Amrita Bindu* (the nectar point) is the indestructible drop beyond the *Atman*. The point comes, and then the circle, then the point inside the triangle is the first stable form. The point is always in the center, the center of the heart, the *bindu* is truth. It is important to be satisfied with one's lot. The one who overcomes oneself is mighty in body, mind, and spirit.

Birth Bestows Life. Death Repairs Life.

Revealed Secrets of Psychological and Spiritual and Material Formation: Their Functions in the Interim and Extreme Human Life

Three things in the growth process form the basis of life: from the embryo to the fetus and to the formation of a human form, with all the limbs and internal organs in the womb. When birth takes place, the infant thinks only minimally after a month or so, [and] significant growth processes outside the womb begin. Three categories of the growth process include the physical, or morphological, the biological, and the mental. The physical growth process is natural. The biological plunges the child into a development process. The child acquires its impressions by contact and the charismatic apparatus that is hidden within the seed of unknown factors such as emotions, alignment, and attitudinal gross impacts. The third category is mental, which is hard to pinpoint until the child can walk and talk, maybe at the age of four or five. The physical growth outside the womb may be rapid, normal, or subdued. These factors depend upon the impact the child experiences by coming into contact with parents, acquaintances, friends, and the family atmosphere.

Somehow, all three growth trends stem from the embryonic experience and individual characteristics that are influenced by internal and external phases of evolvement and involvement. The factors in the psyche of a child may be called the internal emancipated evolutionary vortexes that spin and toil towards external progressive forces. The child's impressions from associated factors of the world around and from the people who take interest in the child, especially parents, brothers, and sisters, make what may be called the developmental attitudinal expression of the child in its activities and actualization. A walking child becomes a mocking child as it totters and tumbles, at a time when the child is generally called the apple of the mother's eye or the father's smile. This continues till the child grows up to eight years, when biological changes play an important part in the makeup of the psyche. Related factors also come into play, such as conscious activities, as well as unknown factors that cannot be comprehended even by very closely related persons. All these depend upon the physical growth and the biological seeding, but the growing child is accustomed to being sheltered and protected from prejudice, perversion, and adverse environmental related conditions and coordinating impulses, which come from within and without. The child grows physically in the natural sense, but mentally there is a sequence of instabilities and insecure feelings.

This is the time when the paramount duty of the parents is to nurture the growing child psychologically, biologically, and physically. The triple assets of any growth process are a guarded secret and could never be divulged to the critical eye of the society. This is called the home life, which contains and sustains incentives that meander between good and bad. The loftiest mind is self-made. If a child is given opportunity and an atmosphere of gaiety and joy, there comes a time when the growing child enters the teenage group. Proper education and acculturation, self-respect, self-confidence, and (an element of) security, sanity and substantiality, bred into a cohesive progressive interactive exuberant mode, plays a very important part in the moods of the growing child. At this stage, the attitude of the growing child is very important. Distractions and detractions are to be avoided. This gives an impetus to the inner growth, which has a definite bearing on the external and modified circumstances. Growth of the mind and growth of the body should progress together to achieve a profound result. Study and self-analysis are necessary to perpetuate a perfect base or a launching pad in the world at large. Admit mistakes unequivocally. Make no excuses. Affirmation, adequate understanding of all the currents of life, adjustment of mental attitude, and physical strength are all advisable factors relating to the progress as an individual and as a connected being to the emotional and spiritual factors. Spirituality should be at the base of all indoctrination. Self-study is the [examination] of the self and related factors that keep one intact without being swayed away by extraneous factors inherent in the atmosphere of the world. 'Come what may' is not an admirable attitude but a tendency towards arrogance and defeatism.

The world is a field of variety, enchantment, attraction, distraction, and detraction. These factors may lead to fragmentation of the psyche of the growing person. Life is full of episodes, events, bends and turns, ups and downs, mirth and joy, happiness and sorrow. Moreover, some fragments (of all the fragments) may be sidetracked in the world at large. It is therefore necessary to strengthen the base and the basic principle of solidarity, oneness, and unchanging individuality. Up to the stage of adolescence, there is no element of ego in the growing child. The adult stage is reached approximately at the age of twenty-two. If the growing person is not influenced by the vagaries of the destructive world, adult life would grow into a life of integrity, which may influence the internal atmosphere, provided for in a sumptuous way at a prior growth stage, probably between four and seven years. Here is the test of the parental ability to keep the child's mind unpolluted and unassailed. In all these stages, including adulthood, the person then develops no political propensity, drug culture, or isolation.

July 14, 2005

A true master showers love from the depths of the heart.
Dr. Shyam's boundless love and patience
had no end.

Figure 17

The Teaching of the "ATIONS"

> SEX IS MULTIPLICATION, IT NEEDS SANCTIFICATION
> SENSES NEED GRATIFICATION AND MORTIFICATION
> INTELLECT NEEDS SUBLIMATION
> INTELLIGENCE NEEDS RATIFICATION
> MIND NEEDS MYSTIFICATION
> HEART NEEDS JUSTIFICAITON
> SPIRIT NEEDS LOVE AND GLORIFICATION
> LOVE NEEDS FORTIFICATION
> FRIENDSHIP NEEDS CLARIFICATION
> DESIRES NEED NULLIFICATION
> IGNORANCE NEEDS FALSIFICATION
> LIFE NEEDS PACIFICATION
> PROBLEMS NEED SIMPLIFICATION

The body has five senses, called the Sense Sensorium.

SEX IS MULTIPLICATION and NEEDS SANCTIFICATION. Senses need gratification but ultimately go Godward where they do not need anything else. For this reason, senses need mortification. We suffer because we are carried away to pacify the itch in the brain. This is the reason we don't achieve something very high. There are points in the brain where it itches and we then suffer because of attractions.

SANYAMA is the term in Sanskrit for how we are ruined if we go on indulging in those things.

DHYANA is the awareness that "in giving, we receive."

SADHASEVIVEKA is true discrimination; truthfully oriented discrimination which understands.

MORTIFICATION of the senses is needed in going Godward; we have to control our mind and our senses.

Sex needs SANCTIFICATION of the impulses versus becoming a pimp to oneself, which is the greatest blunder to oneself. In the world, sex is a quick fix. (But it is an actual energy of creation, therefore arising from the *Sanctum Sanctorum*.) We cannot enter the temple until we take a bath, and take our shoes off. This is purification of the heart and mortification of the body. Thoughts need to see the beautiful womb of creation. Otherwise they can cause biochemical disorders, leading to depression and vicious thinking. The origin of thought is the senses. Love can bring up our thinking in a righteous way. A fit of passion can obstruct our thoughts. We need a bit of caution, not to starve the senses but to regularize them. The senses need gratification, a higher purpose. Senses need the gratification that will bring a permanent happiness. Then one sense does not overpower the others.

INTELLECT NEEDS SUBLIMATION: the intellect is a product of living conditions. It is the source of arrogance. For it to be sublimated, the person must embark on a profound onward journey to be rendered sublime rather than arrogant. When sublimated, there is not an ego problem. The intellect is mechanical and can do mechanical work.

INTELLIGENCE NEEDS RATIFICATION: When we think about and try to correct ourselves, it requires intelligence rather than intellect. Intelligence is wisdom, the highest gift of the gods.[2]

MIND NEEDS MYSTIFICATION: The mind has wavelike formations, which are like cloud formations. Every mystic is a mind-born person.

HEART NEEDS JUSTIFICATION: The heart can be misplaced or displaced. *Hridaya* or the heart of God is a mysterious, classified secret of God. If the heart cannot justify, it cannot do. It cannot cut life or actions into pieces. The heart and brain belong to the whole person. The heartbeat is the beat of creation. The heart only can justify our actions, if they are right or wrong.

SPIRIT NEEDS LOVE AND GLORIFICATION: We can sense it.

LOVE NEEDS FORTIFICATION: Love is the abundance of yourself. Love does not want anything. Make it strong and sturdy so it does not waver. We know it is faulty if it slips or slaps. Love is sober, somber, and affectionate. If love is there, we do not fall.

FRIENDSHIP NEEDS CLARIFICATION: When love attracts, it pulls. We can clash with each other, but it brings you out. It is not the attraction of externals but of Divine qualities.

DESIRES NEED NULLIFICATION: If we go on fulfilling desires, we end up in debt.

IGNORANCE NEEDS FALSIFICATION: We must falsify its existence to become intelligent.

LIFE NEEDS PACIFICATION: otherwise it becomes irritated, angry, hopeless. Life is eternal. We create conditions and call them life. Then we condemn ourselves.

PROBLEMS NEED SIMPLIFICATION: Simplify life, otherwise we go on brooding.

The tenets of true religion are to bring us back, to bind us back to the Creator.

Teach children, "Your life is not in vain, not a waste. Your life is a fertile beautiful substratum." Human beings have to open to life with a concentrated act of perfection without perfidy. We create conditions. We get married and make a condition. Marriage brings suffering or joy. It can be a thought-filled aggrandizement and then turns to aggravation, oppression, and depression. It depends upon how you treat yourself, in a rightful direction or not.

Children can bring suffering or joy or both. Mind acts as an intervener, if we have a good base. We must have a suitable attitude to the enlightenment of life. There is nothing like enlightenment unless you lighten yourself. Enlightenment is a light. The psyche is a capsule holding all the answers and all the things you have done. Life is an eternal flow and you are in it. You can get yourself drowned or swim across.

Love, as we use it, is a byproduct of vicious thinking. As long as there is a trace of selfishness; it is not love. Intelligence needs ratification, verification, and rectification. Intellect creates monsters. Intelligence dissolves these so we see ourselves as we are. If we see our faces in a mirror, the intellect thinks, "How beautiful am I."

The mind is unconscious; it should remind us of consciousness. What is the mind? Who experiences who? The mind needs mystification and to enjoy mystification. Otherwise the brain chatters all the time.

---

[2] It is an endowment of the Cosmic Mind. To see the complete resulting progression of our attitudes and actions needs intelligence. This is beyond the concretizing of the intellect. (Editor)

The heart needs justification, both the organ and the mystical heart. Divine grace is in the heart and justifies everything we come into contact with. It justifies according to our actions. It impartially judges the self, but we cannot as long as the mind interferes.

The spirit needs love and glorification; just love is everywhere. Jesus had a dove on his left shoulder. The heart is connected by channels to the left shoulder. The liver is connected to the right shoulder.

Love needs fortification as a glorious aspect of the Divine, which confers all blessings upon us. The food of Spirit is love.

A talk at a retreat, July 8, 2007

Chapter VI

=====

STHITAPRAJNA - TO BE ESTABLISHED IN THE SELF, THE FOUNDATION OF ALL CONDUCT

*Everyone is unique. Every human being has a star. Know yourself first.
Develop discriminative power. Even your own shadow changes every day.
You cannot surpass anyone.*

*God gives you some kind of light to read your mind and heart.
Its guarantee is steadfastness and establishment in the order of the law of nature and God.
It saves you from all calamities.*

*Sthitaprajna is to be established in the Self:
"One whose mind is not shaken by adversity, who does not hanker after happiness, who
has become free from blind attachment, fear and anger, is indeed the muni or sage of
steady wisdom." Bhagavad Gita 2:56*

*Human life is a trial period. The progression of human life has to go forward. It cannot stop. It
goes to its destination, unhindered by thought, which can interfere with your progress and evoke
pettiness, dragging you back. We must succeed, pass, perform, and perfect to live in and traverse
the path of impunity without blame. Not to blame someone keeps you above circumstances.
Truth holds and uplifts life to a Divine level.
Then life becomes blameless.
When your thinking knows, you have progressed to infinity.*

*Put a seed in your heart. It grows and becomes beautiful with all colors, a spectrum.
Then you lead a life of glory, transcending pettiness and clumsiness. Your feelings
come from the highest point of life, with millions of lights to light your path.*

*There is an unconfined plane that binds human beings together. It is a vast space not a confined
space. In the earth lies a seed. The original human being is the kernel inside the seed.
The earth confirms upon us the finest of purposes.*

It is the never sleeping cosmic power that protects without draining.
Here we stand unvanquished.
Dignity is the Divine glow. It overtakes at every step.

Illumination is the culmination of the spiritual being.
It is an insoluble salvation that cannot be dissolved.

Shyam
remained true
to his
reverence
for all faiths
and all of life
throughout
his years
in the
United States
as well as
his beloved
India.

Figure 18

To be Established in Your Self is to Establish in Self-awareness

To surrender to the Highest Principle is the way beyond conflict. We postpone everything. Lack of surrender is psychological complexity implemented by an egoistic attitude. Avoid this attitudinal imperialism. Pride does not allow a person to surrender. As long as you feel you have a choice, you haven't surrendered. A vulnerable person succumbs to temptation and falls into a contrived state of conditioning. A nincompoop is a tyrannically stressful, erratically blissful person. Gullibility is the state of innocence of a baby. Such innocence and beauty must be taught to be good and strong. When you are above ignorance, you do not make a choice. You rise above. You are guided by magnanimity and intelligence. *Sthitaprajna* is the ability to fortify your Self to become strong and steadfast, with a Divine purpose behind you. The Divine is limitless exuberance, compassion, and the highest intelligence. The above is there in the bottom of your heart.

Everybody has at least two personalities, negative and positive. You cannot be real because you have not recognized yourself. Self-abnegation is to diminish the linkage you have to the Divine process, limitless exuberance, and compassion. Compassion is not a compromising passion.

You can overcome the negative by the positive, once you ascertain these. Then you surrender to the noble personality that is good, charitable, equitable, and most pleasing. It helps you cross the ocean of life. Rising above is progress. To rise above your foibles and pettiness is to make your life a grand finale. The heart dwells in the Self. The mind becomes immortal, and the body becomes sustainable. Once you build up the positive personality, like Gandhi and other great leaders, it is indomitable.

This careful attitude helps you to proceed with your life in a noble way. Everyone needs to realize that this negative personality has caused great harm. You overpower the negative personality by jumping on its head like *Krishna* who jumped on top of the poisonous serpent in the Yamuna River. Then your listening is not to submit to false values. You fuse with right action. You crucify your infirmities, shortcomings, bad habits, doubtful nature, and then you are rejuvenated, resurrected, and you ascend.

Rising above is progress; otherwise life is the same dirty sham. If you want to succeed, establish yourself in your Resplendent God Self. Then in cremation, the god *Agni* will enjoy the goodness of the person, "I will not burn him, but hold him on the tongue of the flame." The light must be your delight. Light brought intelligence into the world. Intelligence is equal to the Divine dispensation. The light comes from the breath of God.

To lighten your burdens, lighten your mind. This gives a spiral light to all your activities. It will ennoble people to modify their lives.

The burden of proof is with the expansive consciousness.

Your actions prove who you are and who you are not.

If you don't develop your character, you will not see the truth.

Chapter VII

THE BASIC TRINITY OF CONDUCT

First, Right Food - Ahara
Second, Right Recreation - Vihara
Third, Right Behavior - Achara
All branches of knowledge come from these three:
Right understanding and their use leads to tranquility of mind.

The enemies of the Self are carnal lust, anger and wrath, intoxication, jealousy and envy, along with covetousness, with greed and avarice. These enemies are the machine to measure your mental caliber. Even greed to amass wealth can have a good purpose if it is used for a good purpose. Intelligence is necessary! Each enemy even has a therapeutic value in a certain measure, but beyond that measure, they ruin and obstruct the connection to the Divine Self. The highest level of ego is not much ego because the ego is sublimated. Everything you have is for testing yourself.

Life is a lyric. It depends upon who writes the lyric and who abides by it. The real lyric was written long ago at the dawn that was the demise of time.

You need a good immune system, a good way of life, a good habit of eating, a good habit of repose and sleeping. Those are the good ingredients that go into forming a real human being who is inseparable from the Godhead.

Ayurveda and the Basic Trinity of Conduct

Buddhavidya is the science of mind and the science of elements. The human psyche is a powerful container of psychological, functional factors that become a useful tool in treating mental ailments attributed to wrong doing. A psychologist or a psychiatrist (*Bhutavidya*) is supposed to have the knowledge of the creative elements connected to nature and its amplification in each and every life, which is considered to be the glorious beginning and ending of a longevity process. It consists of three Basic Principles that mean "to be good and do good."

The basic trinity of conduct is: Right Food, Right Recreation, and Right Behavior. All branches of knowledge come from these three. They lead to tranquility of mind. These principles of *Ayurveda*, the science of life, treat the conditions of life and also promote the profound knowledge of longevity, which enables a person to be useful in long and healthful service to the human race.

1. Right Food (*Ahara*) is very important to the human body. You must understand yourself. From eating good food for eight days, the mind will be calm and cool. Food should be sumptuous and suitable to develop all the senses in a rightful way.
2. Right Recreation (*Vihara*) means to be attuned to nature, as the trees sway - from the movements of nature, dance came into being: from a beautiful breeze, blooming flowers, flowing water, rippling sounds of water (ocean). Life in harmony is devotional dance; absorption is devotion. Bharta *(Arjuna in the Mahabharata)* started dance in India. It was a response to inspiration from nature.

A wonderful therapy is to walk on blades of green grass.

3. Right Behavior (*Achara*) is behavioral psychology. Psychology is the study of the psyche. Behavioral development comes by discriminating between *sadchara*, good conduct, and *durachara*, bad conduct, which may turn into an enemy in the body and hurt the individual and the universal.

After the basic principles are achieved by constant vigilance and intercession, the process of life becomes easier, healthier, and conducive to proper living and compassionate approaches toward all creatures, small and big. The creation then becomes a force of energy conducive to the upliftment, peace, prosperity, and advancement of the sole aim of life that is spiritual and moral tenants of oneness, and to achieve the unified field of existence.

Yoga means to yoke yourself to goodness, yoke yourself to God. To be God-based is to be broad-based. We are not broad because of territorial locality with manifested accumulated energies.

God is weightless. [When giving yourself to God] going up is easier and easier—you become lighter. Resistance to going up is ego. We create a vault inside of ourselves and live in that to maintain our identity. The false worldly personality is provoked by ambition and the desire to maintain identity. We lose the capacity to surrender. Lassitude with clinging, anger, desire, greed—weighs you down. These are intrinsic in life activities, but an excess of the above comes from ignorance. Attachment is fear. To accumulate in life is OK, but don't be attached to it. If you are attached, you will suffer a lot. Don't get attached to the idea, "I think I am so and so." It is OK to think of it, but not to be attached to the false "I." Then you'll lift your hand to the flow of life and give to the earth, which gives sustenance in return. Give your heart to your fellow beings.

In this rich, wonderful life, which has come from the grace of God, human beings have gone astray. Without the grace of God, we cannot even lift a blade of grass.

Satsang Talk, June 6, 2006

In this rich, wonderful life,
which has come from
the grace of God,
human beings have gone astray.

There are 3 Basic Principles summed up as "be good and do good."
The basic trinity of conduct is Food, Recreation, and Behavior.
All branches of knowledge come from these three and lead to tranquility of mind.

1. Food (ahara) is very important to the human body. You must understand yourself.
From eating good food for 8 days, the mind will be calm and cool.
With a balanced diet, we do not need drugs. The mind is conditioned by protein, carbohydrates.
While eating pure food, it is best to not overeat, and generally not to talk.
Wild animals know what to eat; they are highly sensitive and don't fall sick.
Food has a great influence upon the mind. It is the essence of the human being.
2.. Good recreation (vihara) is to be attuned to nature, as the trees sway—dance came into
being. Inspiration comes from a beautiful breeze, blooming flowers, flowing water, and the
rippling sound of water (ocean). Walk on blades of grass!
Dance in India was a response to inspiration from nature.
3. Behavior (achara) is behavioral psychology and the study of the psyche.

Figure 19

First in the Trinity: Right Food – *Ahara*

Food is made by pure consciousness. It is considered Ishwar *(God).*

Food has a great influence upon the mind; it is the essence of the human being.

Cooking is a holy undertaking.

If you take a good look at exactly how much and what you eat, you will find your proper measure. If you eat the right combinations of food in the right measure, you will not go into depression. Food itself can be an oppressor.

When cooking is done taking the name of God, it helps others be good. We feed the God within us.

The food of Spirit is love.

Food has a Great Influence Upon the Mind; It is the Essence of the Human Being

Food is very important to the human body. The land at present is so depleted. Its potency is not the same. The nutritional value of food is not the same. The poison in the earth is translated into poisons in the brain that then goes helter-skelter. You must understand yourself: What parts build up the nervous system, the endocrine system, and all the systems. The mind is conditioned by protein, fats, and carbohydrates. Broadly I'll tell you what is good to eat: lots of grains, a lot of vegetables... 60% of grains, 30% of vegetables, and 10% of proteins. In the ancient times, people didn't think about vitamins and minerals. Their senses were so sensitive they could really understand what to eat.

From eating good food for eight days, the mind will be calm and cool. With a balanced diet, we do not need drugs. While eating pure food, it is best to not overeat, and generally not to talk. Wild animals know what to eat; they are highly sensitive and don't fall sick.

We offer our food to God before we eat. You can have the conviction that the God eats this food because the God is in me.

Here is a grace given to us in the great epic, the *Mahabharata*:

Brahmarpanam Brahma Havir Brahma Gnou Brahmana Hutam
Brahaiva Tena Gantavyam Brahma Karma Samadhina

Translated as: *Brahman* (the Supreme) is the oblation or ritual, *Brahman* is the offering, *Brahman* is the One sacrificing Itself in Its own fire to that is *Brahman*, verily *Brahman* is reached only by the one who always sees *Brahman* in action.

But what does God really eat? He eats the goodness. He partakes of the goodness in everybody and blesses them to be good continuously. We have faith that we offer the food to God symbolically and that the food will be blessed. Along with food comes God's blessing.

The food of Spirit is love.

We are so closely connected to nature and its varieties of products, which have not been tested or thought about … Eat good food, and enjoy the resonance. Eating goes into the stomach, and the food does its work and feeds the brain. It is so simple, so devoted.

We must be very respectful of the food we eat. That food sustains us and also helps to improve our lives. Therefore, we say, eat food in silence, with great reverence and attention, and that food sustains you. When once you resonate with nature, you find you are in tune with the entire nature, including the solar rays, which have the photons. The electrons in your system, the food you eat, resonates with that photon and captures it, makes a beautiful electromagnetic wave. Everything is myself. There are planetary lei lines corresponding to lei lines in our own bodies. The microcosm is the macrocosm. It means that whatever is in you is in the universe. Once you have that wave, you are in harmony with everything. Why is it so hard to do that?

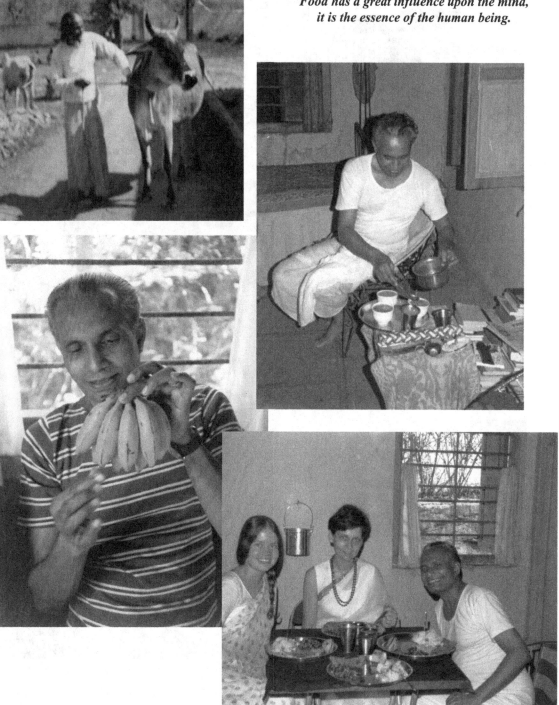

The food of Spirit is love.
The inability to take care
brings anarchy.

Food has a great influence upon the mind,
it is the essence of the human being.

Figure 20

65

*When you think of food, think,
"Someone has to cook my food,
it might as well be me".*

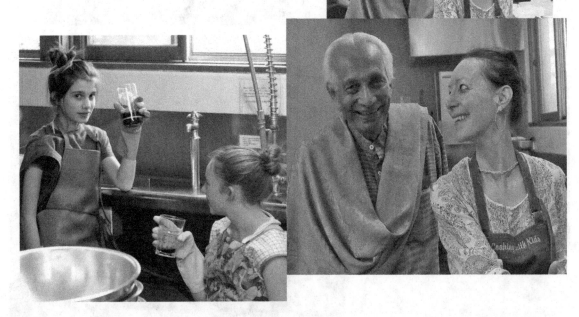

Figure 21

Second in the Trinity: Right Recreation - *Vihara*

Memories of Fun and Joyful Sharing

Humor is a basic principle.
Creativity comes out of conflict.
In music and dance, the Supreme dances in our heart all the time.

It sings in your heart because our soul is a song of the Divine.

The yearning for the Divine brings forth a life in harmony. Absorption is devotion.
This one-pointed devotion is a yearning for deliverance. The movements that go
into the system are all mixed, coordinated, and harmonious in absorption.

There is a kind of movement in nature from sunrise until sunset that is the absorption of
devotion. This yearning is not an ordinary thing. It is a movement of nature itself.

The soul is the song of God. So this Divine dances in your heart all the time. Therefore
He created this world, according to East Indians, to enjoy it. He wants to enjoy your
heart, your mind, your soul, everything. He wants to enjoy without sacrificing Himself,
but giving everything to you, and also without polluting you. See, that's God.

Everybody has some talents.
God gives them to us to make use of them.
By doing so, we pay them back to God.
Long ago, Sage Kashyapa said whatever
your talents and potentials,
make use of them.
You send back your gratitude when you make use of
them. You are helping His creation.
You try to get to a point equal to something higher
and have created that Higher Principle inside you.

Figure 22

Some of Shyam's Favorite Stories

It is Possible to be Unified and Have All Support

I. The story of *Tukaram* shows how we need no other support but the all-support of the cosmic power. He was a poor saint who had a family, a wife, and eight children. His only means of support was to take the name of God, *Panduranga*. He could never keep a job but finally was hired to drive away the birds in a field of crops. Everyone, his employer and his family and friends, criticized him for his "inactivity." The birds listened while he sang the name of God all day, and they left the field alone. It prospered and gave abundant crops. Finally, the whole village recognized what he had done.

II. *Tulsidas*, a powerful singer who could move the elements, was in love with a beautiful girl. One day the king asked him to come into his court and show his power of sound to all. The girl could not enter, so she had to stay outside. *Tulsidas* dazzled the court with his powers to move all the elements and natural principles. Then the king asked him to invoke *Agni*, the god or principle of fire. As *Tulsidas* sang, he started to burn and eventually caught flame. His beloved heard of this to her immense distress. She then started to sing a song for *Vayu*, the waters and rain. With this song empowered by the great force of her love, she quenched the flames devouring her beloved.

III. *Savitri* was a beautiful and virtuous princess who was to find a husband, according to the customs of the day. Many princes came to court her, but none did she find suitable. Her parents allowed her to travel through the countryside. One day she saw a beautiful lad who shone like the sun. From another kingdom, he was a deposed prince from a takeover of court politics, and he and his parents lived in exile in the forest. There was, furthermore, a curse set upon him that he would die on his sixteenth birthday. In spite of this, *Savitri* insisted on marriage to him, and they lived happily for a short time. All effort was exerted to keep the prince safe from harm. Sadly though, he was bitten by a poisonous snake and lay dying in *Savitri's* arms. The god of death, *Yama*, came to take away his soul, but *Savitri*, through the power of her own penance and virtue, followed *Yama*, who told her she had to turn back. *Savitri* was persistent and *Yama* respected that, so he told her she could ask for three boons and then she had to go back. She then asked if her father's blindness could be cured. *Yama* replied "done." She next asked that her father's kingdom would prosper. *Yama* replied, "Done." Then she asked if her father would live to see his grandchildren. *Yama* said, enthusiastically, knowing this was the third boon, "Done!" *Savitri* asked him, "How will my father see his grandchildren if my husband is dead?" *Yama*, who had never been stumped by any mortal, was outwitted by a young woman. He returned the prince to life. Thus is the power of a virtuous woman!

IV. Jewish prisoners in Auschwitz put God on trial. Having a great dispute with God, they tried God "in absentia." They presented all the views, all the pros and cons, and ultimately they convicted God. Afterward they said to each other, "Now let us go and pray." You can continue to quarrel with God, but faith brings you together.

V. A great priest was teaching for thirty years in a church. One day he died and went to heaven. And there was a taxi driver, a cab driver. In heaven, they had given him a great golden car. And this priest got a tiny silver one. He was worried about it. He mentioned it to Peter, "I preached all my life, and I have this tiny silver car, and this cab driver, what would he have done? See? He has a huge golden car!" Peter said, "We go by results here. All the people slept while you preached. The cab driver, when he was driving, they prayed!"

VI. *Gorakumbar* was a famous potter. People went to him for spiritual advice. One day a well-known pundit came to him asking, "Why do these people listen to him and not to me?" The potter took his tool and hit the pundit on the head. "This one is not baked," he said. When the ego is not sublimated, surrendered, noble, simple, and equi-local, the sanity and steadiness is not established. The humble person knows more. The ocean is four inches below all the rivers.

VII. A robber was following a man who ran away and disappeared. The man came to the home of a sage who let him hide there. The robber came soon after and asked the sage, "Have you seen a man passing through here?" The sage replied, "No one passed through here." The man was saved by the precision of truth. God's truth is a double edged sword and has a wide berth.

VIII. *Akbar* and his minister had a previous lifetime together. They were starving and people brought them *chapattis*. The minister ate before sharing with others. *Akbar*... shared his food first, before eating. This spirit to share helped *Akbar* become the emperor in his next life. Sharing is sublimation of the ego. Arising from a vast ancestry, this generosity of the heart is different from a contraction of the heart.

IX. *Valmiki* was a great sinner. He attacked, murdered, and robbed people on the road and took all their wealth to feed and support his family. One day he aggressively approached the great sage *Narada*, who told *Valmiki*, "I don't have anything for you! But let me ask you one thing. With all the booty you bring to your family, why not ask them if they will share this terrible *karma* with you?" *Valmiki* went home and asked his wife, then his children. No one said they would share the *karma*, in spite of enjoying the wealth. *Valmiki* returned to *Narada* who was waiting for him. "They will not share my *karma*." *Narada* said, "Then you must save yourself from your sins. Say the name of God and you will be released." Being so evil, *Valmiki* could not even pronounce the name of *Ram*, so *Narada* said, "Then say the name of *Mara* (the evil one) and over time it will become *Ram*." *Valmik's* supplication was so intense; a molehill grew up around him. Finally, released from his sin through his wholehearted austerity, *Valmiki* received a boon from *Narada* to be able to write the great Indian epic, the *Ramayana*.

X. *Draupadi*, a noble queen in the epic the *Mahabharata*, was dragged into a full courtroom and humiliated. The evil rulers wanted to disrobe her. Her only recourse was to pray to God, to Lord *Krishna*, raising her arms and supplicating, "Oh my God, save me!" As they pulled her sari, it kept increasing in length and she remained clothed. Finally, the man pulling her sari fell down in a heap himself. This is surrender, to be naked in front of God, and to be saved from calamity. When in great difficulty, the mind is sober. Otherwise, it drinks the wine of the ego.

Calamity can aid in the process of universal growth. In surrender, the "I" is sublimated to, "I am that principle called God. I am the essence of God."

XI. Another story of *Draupadi* was also one of Shyam's favorites. After she and the *Pandava* brothers were exiled from their own kingdom, their evil cousin *Duryodhana* still wanted to harass them while they struggled to survive in the forest. *Duryodhana* sent a wrathful sage *Durvasa* and his multitude of followers to visit the *Pandavas* and ask for food. *Draupadi* was panicked and only prayed for Lord *Krishna* to help. Instantly, He walked in the door and begged for food. *Draupadi* said, "I have nothing!" But *Lord Krishna* insisted asking her to show him the empty pots. One had a tiny bit of vegetable that evaded washing. He took that one sliver and burped loudly. At that moment, *Durvasa* and his followers were stricken with terrible stomach pains and diarrhea. To see if they wanted food, the *Pandava* brothers approached them at the riverside, where they'd been cleansing themselves. They all ran away in agony. The teaching of this story is that when the Lord is satisfied, everyone must be satisfied - unless their greed overtakes them.

XII. Lord *Buddha's* death was preceded by His taking an offering of contaminated food. In India, a guest is treated as God. So when the devotee offered, *Buddha* did not decline. As He was dying, the devotee was weeping and sorrowful. *Buddha* blessed him, thanked him, and told him to have no grief because the devotee provided Him the way for His liberation.

XIII. A devout practitioner was caught on top of his roof in a terrible flood. He had no way to rescue himself but thought, "My God will save me!" First some people in a small motorboat drove by and offered him a ride. He refused, saying, "My God will save me!" A while later, a helicopter flew overhead and threw down a line. The man shouted, "No thank you, my God will save me!" Finally, a small canoe came by, and the people also offered to pick him up. Again, the man refused, "My God will save me!" He perished in the flood. When he went up to heaven, he asked God, "Why didn't you save me?" Impatiently, the Lord said, "I tried, you fool! I sent you a motorboat, a helicopter, and a canoe!"

XIV. A father had several sons. The oldest became very successful and made lots of money. Another was not so successful but was very righteous. When they each came face to face with God, they were asked, "What did you leave in your will?" The eldest said, "I left my children lots of money." The other brother said, "I left my children the value of life."

And one of Shyam's favorite modern jokes:
Moses was exhausted and went to God. He had headaches and unending troubles with his people. God said, "Moses, why is your face so shallow and peaked?" Moses explained that his people were in dire straits. They were worshiping idols and turned violent and licentious. He was at a loss what to do. God looked at him with great love, "It will be all right Moses, take two tablets and go to bed!"

Everything is myself.
Whatever is in you is in the universe.

Figure 23

Where there is love, there is the heart.
Where there is love and heart, there is God.
Where there is God, there is peace
and tranquility. Where there is peace and
tranquility, there is unending creation.
Where there is unending creation, there is
super recreation. Where there is super
recreation, there is joy. Where there is joy,
there is eternal life. Where there is eternal life,
there is paradise. Where there is paradise,
there is immense happiness,
With no strings attached!

Figure 24

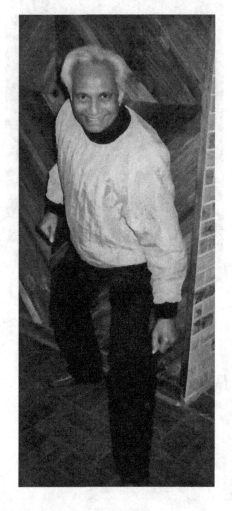

*The real function of relationship leads to the
flowering of humane humanity in each
and every human being,
within the profound silence of the Immeasurable.*

*Generally, people hang out, but they don't hang in.
It's good to hang in.*

Figure 25

Third in the Trinity: Right Behavior- *Achara*

*Right behavior is to follow the path of truth. Making your moral fiber strong,
it spreads throughout the universal attitude and altitude.*

*Character is one of the emblems of a human being. It brings the diamond of fortitude
and the pearl of softness. It never culminates but goes on to the
threshold of time and the rim of existence.*

*Moral life is real life. Complexity ruins morality.
Righteousness is a silent virtue. It doesn't advertise itself.*

Be like the Chataka *bird that waits for water from the rain
and does not drink from low-lying water.*

*Without character, it is not worth living in the world.
We boast but not boost our inner morality.
Redemption comes from discipline. Responsibility is to meet every situation adequately.
Discipline gives you the self-confidence and strength to face any problem.
It is a discipleship to the Self.*

A human being with no gratitude is worse than an animal.

The criterion for spiritual progress is gratitude, even for difficult times.

That which releases me from worldly woe is not my foe.

*Wisdom will test you to see how long you will stand its tests
and hold yourself infallible, how well you are established in your own Self.*

Don't be a slave to your whims and fancies. Be a master of them.

*If the tests fail before you, it shows you are established in wisdom.
You will see your Self in your own Light.*

The key to open the door is the Dharma, *that which will hold you up to extent of your
capacity to be good. Be good, do good. Do what you love, love what you do.
We live in our deeds. Good deeds are rewarded by our own Self, enabling the person
to reach the Higher Planes as well as the Ultimate.
Surrender to your noble personality.*

How do you divide a sky? There is nothing like a Hindu, Buddhist, or Christian. We have made a dire calamity. There is no greater calamity than to be discontented in one's lot. Be grateful and contented with what God has given you. A tree has hundreds of branches, but they do not fight each other. The sun never says to the earth, "You owe me." There is just One God. There is no division between.

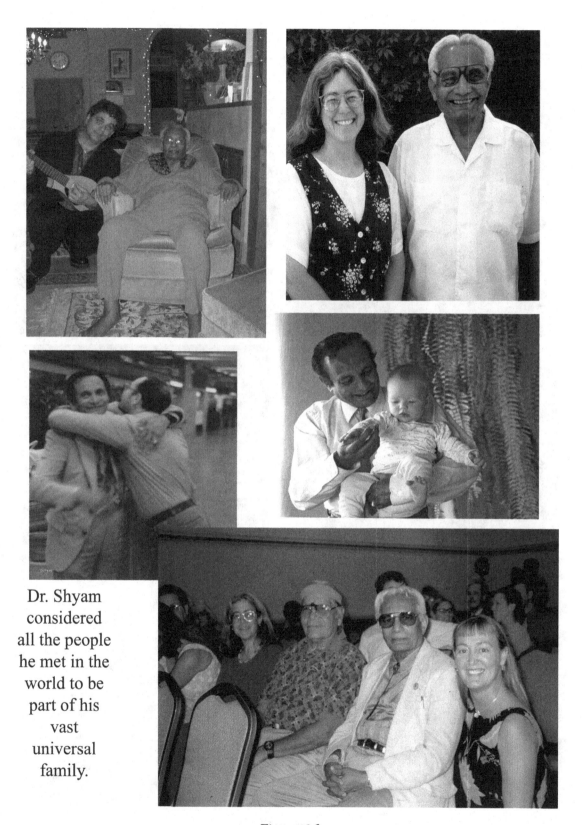

Dr. Shyam
considered
all the people
he met in the
world to be
part of his
vast
universal
family.

Figure 26

One
big
and
pretty
happy
family
too.

Figure 27

Right Worship as Part of Right Behavior - *Achara*

The East is spiritual. The West is political. In the middle are the ways of morality.

Every time you worship, the Divine is born and born and born. So you are the Creator of God. You must know that. You're the Creator of God. God is your Creator. You are the Creator of God also. That's creation. It's not co-creation, which sounds like co-conspirators! It is creation. Therefore, in the end, what happens is that there is no difference between the Creator and the Created. They're all One.

In 2012, there was a magnetic shift in the earth. Internally the axis and gravitational forces shifted. Human beings have lost their natural connection to nature, and some cannot handle these changes. A comet passed by Jupiter and turned it into a computer to supply unknown information from the unknown. Scientists will become spiritually oriented. This energy changed our brain chemistry and will produce a high caliber reception in the brain.

Calamity can be a spiritual process.

Mantras can foster the process of universal growth. Say the name in a smooth, submissive way. The correct pronunciation of a mantra gives a double dose of spiritual energy.

We sing to be righteous, to be frank to ourselves. Otherwise we cannot be good to others.

Sing your chants and mantras, and the mind will not be vicious. All these chants can be recited at any time of the day, in whatever mood you are: It doesn't matter whether you are in an ordinary mood, or a defiant mood, or a refined mood.

Chanting mantras gives a noble stature to the brain and your brain cells will travel beyond you. In chanting mantras, you cook the brain on the sacrificial fire of life.

Practice of Mantras[3]

Mantram come from seed roots of sound. Not invented, they are revelations from the Divine. Every Mantra has a particular healing energy associated with cosmic principles of formation through sound. The syllables, words, and intonations work on the cellular and subatomic levels. Working from the inside out, they restore potentiality and rearrange cosmic matter. When *Mantram* is sincerely practiced, it works on the level of creation, penetrating up to seven barriers and restoring seven layers of the human constitution.

On Meditation

Human beings should be aware of every action, totally aware. Watch the mind. Mind that watches the mind. If mind is confused, the confused mind watches. In modern times, when you sit for meditation, you get caught in the methodology of it. When you sit, the mind still chatters. This is not meditation. Meditation is to know the meditator when the meditator is absent. When there is only meditation, not a single thought in the mind, that mind is energy. People say "I can't stop the mind." If you are always aware, giving total attention to whatever you do, then what does the mind do? It is attending totally. If the mind merges with the heart, then you encompass the whole world. Real longing is not craving but a longing to do good to this creation; then comes the power of God. You need not be a master of yourself, but don't be a slave of yourself. Be what you are. You are the means to an end, and the end is your means. You are that light, a great column of light through which you can see the entire the universe. You need not go back in time.

---

[3] (Editor's note)

Ramakrishna Paramahansa, Sri Anandamayi Ma, Swami Vivekananda, and many saints and sages, including Dr. Shyam, promoted the practice of Japa, or continually saying the names of God, as well as chanting Mantras as the paramount practice in this dark age of human depravity and confusion. Holy Mantras are received as a transmission of energy from a realized master and given to the devotee as a sacred trust. They create a key to higher and more refined energies in the cosmos and can heal, center, stimulate creative powers, and bring the devotee in alignment with the Divine Self.

A great friend of Shyam's, Sri Anandamayi Ma, gives a beautiful and straightforward explanation of the practice of mantra yoga as worship: "Have firm faith that the seed, which has been buried in your consciousness, will without fail grow into a tree. Just as after sowing a seed, it has to be watered and manured; similarly the seed in the form of a mantra [prayer of sound and power to the deity] will sprout when provided with the necessary nourishment in the form of Satsang [right company]. As you desire God, be it in a particular form or without form, so will you find Him." Matri Vani (Calcutta: Shree Shree Anandamayee Charitable Society, 1982) p.191–192.

In his role as Orthodox Priest
and Hindu Brahman,
Dr. Shyam presided
over many consecrations
of marriage and sacred ritual.

Figure 28

More happy
memories
with
Dr. Shyam's
universal
family.

Figure 29

Spiritual Practice

After creating and creating the gods became intoxicated with their own power. Then the demon became their designated driver!

Many people find it difficult to do spiritual practice in the modern age. In olden days, they had more time to go to the temple, synagogues, and holy places. Nowadays, it is very difficult. Maybe you are busy or you have problems, or both, or you are having problems being busy. What is this spiritual practice in our busy world? It is necessary to do spiritual practice. It is the only thing that will give happiness, peace of mind, and a kind of power that a person can face the world. If you do not have these spiritual practices behind your life, you become very weak and completely exhausted. Then you become insignificant. The world is so vast. Every place you go there is some place beyond it. People often take up spiritual practices out of curiosity. Then you practice for a while, get disgusted, and give it up. For spiritual practice, there is no place, no time.

Suppose when you get up and go to the office that becomes a spiritual practice. You start with whatever beliefs you have. The Hindus say "*Ram, Ram, Ram.*" If a man walks to a mine in the early morning, works all the day, and returns at 7:30 at night, he never says "I am tired." I never found people saying "I'm tired; I'm tired of this world." The whole time he is walking he is saying "*Ram, Ram, Ram.*" There are millions of people who work all day, longs days, in this world, but their religion has given them a hold. When they get out of bed in the morning, they say "*Ram, Ram, Ram.*" When they wash their face in the morning, they say "*Ram, Ram, Ram.*" Some Christians say "Oh Lord." But the only thing is that they don't give it their attention. It is mechanical.

Suppose you concentrate, you sincerely repeat chants, and then it has a benefit. When you do not pay attention to the duty you have, you meet with an accident. That is a spiritual setback. When you meet with an accident, you become disappointed. You may be wounded, hurt, have neck or back pains, stomach pains or your knees hurt. The ancient formula is that you have to have a spiritual life. It will not disbar you from doing anything that is good in the world because then you turn all your actions into a spiritual life. Someone says, "I forget what is the meaning of it all?" It is only that they are not conscious of it. Forgetfulness, disease, deficiency, dysfunction are only not being conscious of yourself. *Nux Moschata* is a homeopathic remedy that puts your present consciousness in a stupor, and then you remember the other, the wakefulness.

What happens is a miscarriage of our understanding. Nothing is born out of it. That is when we become insignificant. I was standing in front of the ocean in Rio de Janero. It is so vast that someone said they felt insignificant. One thing you must know is that you are vaster than the ocean. Your consciousness is connected to the all-pervading Divine consciousness. Your consciousness is already hooked into it. Whatever you do, you may feel insignificant in front of the ocean, but the only thing is that you do not have the humility of the ocean. If you have that humility, then you have the Divine consciousness. All rivers flow into the ocean.

All must, that is their destiny. All human beings must flow into the God Head. That is their destination. We cannot escape from it. Wherever a river originates, it has to flow into the ocean and all the oceans flow into each other. The ocean is so humble and so vast. It is below all the rivers [that] flow into it. That is why even though God is so enormous, all pervading, and eternal, He is so humble. He even decided to reside in an arrogant person! Suppose he said, "This is an arrogant person; I don't want to stay here." That person would be dead. God is in an arrogant person, in a thief. He is there because He is so humble. When I would see persons in Bombay, in the jails, I would ask them, "Why did you become a thief?" The first thing they would say is that it was comparison to an affluent person. They would say to themselves, "He is better off. He can go into shops and get anything." These people couldn't even take care of their families. They would feel so bad. They wouldn't have proper food to eat. Then they would think all the rich people are mocking them. Even when they grew up and went to school, they would feel this comparison with other children bringing their toys and eatables. So in comparison, they would say, "Whatever it is, let me go and commit a crime." This was the origin of thieving.

In a sense, no person is bad; circumstances make a person do bad things. But he thinks it is a good thing; he is a robber against a rich man who is hoarding money. In England, they have so many valuable things in museums. All these antiques are very expensive, but to some, a person, who is newly born, a human being, has no value. Then a person feels insignificant. These dead things in a museum are what have no value. But we don't understand the psychology of it. Rich people commit crimes also, terrible crimes. This is an affluent society, but people are neglected through the inequitable distribution of wealth. This wealth which people enjoy is not man-made, it is God-given, and still we don't share it with someone else.

Spiritual practices bring you the understanding of this. They bring you into the understanding of how miserable is the condition of our neighbor. Then comes the feeling, "I must go and help." Then when you have a spiritual practice, the other things you are doing become insignificant before a starving person. If you have a posh car, it becomes insignificant before a starving person. Outside the Taj Mahal hotel in India were many children. A lot of Arabs with great holdings would go to this hotel. Outside, the street urchins would beg because they had no food. The police would drive them away. I stood in front of the hotel and told the children not to go. The police said they had been asked to get rid of the children by the hotel management. I created a stir. Afterwards, the police never did this again. I told the hotel, "You have so much food that you waste it, you throw it out. Is there a greater criminal than you? Here are people with no food, no protection from the heat, the cold, and the rain."

This is the spiritual life. You become spiritualized when you do spiritual practices. It is not the question of whether you go to the church or to the temple to pray and meditate. This body is the synagogue, the temple, and the worship place. It is the holy place where God resides. You can worship in it wherever you go. God has not taken any money from you, but He has given you this wonderful body. The totality of God's consciousness is in this body, and God goes everywhere with your body. Whether you take it to a bar or to a mountaintop, it is independent of all those things. The God Principle has given you the capacities of intelligence, understanding, discrimination, and it will not interfere. It is all-pervading. It is the Breath of Life, with no iota of arrogance. It is not polluted. You do wrong things, and you suffer. It is still there, it keeps you alive. If we do wrong things, it doesn't suffer. We do. It has nothing to do.

Flowing water is always considered to be pure. People sit on the Ganges bank, and they watch. A lot of things go on. People even throw in dead bodies, but the Ganges flows on. The flowing consciousness of God is what gives you peace of mind when you die. You forget everything when you die. It survives death of the body, the consciousness of the mind. When a person dies, the tunnel becomes the body. There are 72,000 tunnels and you receive your own knowledge at every tunnel. You go into each one. I said, "Hi Dad, I knew You were here. I picked you up." There are gaps between the tunnels that are light. Each has a sun, a synapse. We are the synapses. There is always light at the end of the tunnel.

The awareness survives all the bad things. Is it not our duty to love that which does not interfere with us? People ask, "Why did God not help me not to do something [that] was bad for me?" God will not. He has given you everything you need. He's kept all these understandings as the law. If you transgress the law, you'll suffer.

Consider the condition of the world. Who has created these problems? Human beings can be God. When you really apply yourself with your entire mind, all your heart, all your body, and all your soul, you can know that. It doesn't mean you have to go to the Himalayas. If you build a house with a view, this body will have to go to see it, it will not come to you, that God inside your abode, this beautiful temple, That inside your body, That will not escape. Why don't you escape your viciousness, your folly, your shortcomings, your tyranny, and your cruelty? The spiritual life can show you the contrast. This is what the spiritual practice can do. Then what needs to fall away will fall away.

Satsang Talk, September, 2000

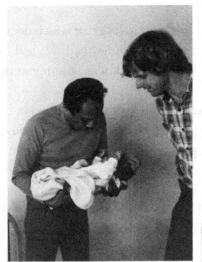

Happy Memories
of
Blessings and Births

Figure 30

Devotion (A Cascade of Quotes)

Your devotion makes you recognize the heart is your temple of loyalty.

The highest human being has inner devotion. People with real devotion are one-pointed, crying from the bottom of their hearts. This is the "cry of the heart." This *bhava,* or devotion, takes away all worldly fear. To go on sincerely chanting removes anger. To sing the name of God all day is to be attractive to the Lord. There are a thousand names.

A true *Bhakta* (devotee) drops the ego. God wants a devotional, selfless approach, not an intellectual approach.

To reach God is to dance to His Heart.

What is God if He doesn't love me? What am I if I don't love Him?

The believers in God have an insoluble salvation that cannot be dissolved. They never care for calamities. Even *Kumbakarna,* the brother of the ferocious demon *Ravenna,* worshiped *Vishnu* and was saved.

The seed of God occupied the womb of Mary, of honest, truthful, and noble heritage. It was a Divine act not a human pact. The Divine can only act through a human being.

What brings God is concentrated devotion, concentrated not extricated. The simple system is taking the name of God. This is how God stands near you and if you fall back, you are pushed forward. If shrinking down, you are made to rise up. If you are fearful, you are made bold. If you are angry, you become calm. If you are hateful, you are made into love. Your psyche is softened.

Transfer all our ignorance to God. He can bear the weight. It's His official capacity! To give Him the burden does not mean passivity.

Bring God to earth because He is a slave to true love. Supplication brings everything to submission, even the God. Joan of Arc had that devotional and emotional facet that saves the human race.

Balancing the beloved requires tremendous energy. God submits to love at the eleventh hour.

We are entrammeled and have imprisoned ourselves in tremendous ways. With devotion, we get a pardon.

In the course of his sojourns in the United States and Brazil, Dr. Shyam blessed many earnest aspirants with a dynamic boost toward Self Realization.

Figure 31

Shyam's Favorite Devotional Prayers of Self-honesty and Supplication

Prayer to Theotokos (Mother of God)[4]

All-holy Lady Theotokos, light of our darkened souls, our hope, our shelter, our refuge, our consolation and our joy, we thank thee that thou hast accounted us worthy, to be the partakers of the immaculate teachings and communion of thy son... Thou, who gavest birth to the true light, enlighten the mental eyes of our hearts. Thou, who did bear the fountain of immortality, quicken our understanding of thy bliss... Compassion-loving Mother of the merciful God... have mercy upon us, grant us humility, contrition of heart, meekness in our thoughts and deliverance from the bondage of our vain imaginings... Account us worthy even unto our last breath to receive... the sanctification of the immaculate mysteries unto the healing of both our souls and bodies...

St. Francis Prayer

Oh Lord, make me an instrument of thy peace.
Where there is hatred, let me sow love;
Where there is injury, pardon; where there is doubt, faith;
Where there is sadness, joy; where there is despair, hope;
And where there is darkness, light.

Oh Divine Master, grant that I may not so much seek to be consoled as to console,
To be understood as to understand,
To be loved as to love.
For it is in giving that we receive,
It is in pardoning that we are pardoned,
And it is in dying that we are born into Eternal Life.

[4] Service Book of the Holy Eastern Orthodox Catholic and Apostolic Church, Antiochian Orthodox Christian Archdiocese of North America, eleventh edition, 2002.

Weddings,
communion
ambrosia,
guidance
and blessings.

Figure 32

In whatever
role he
assumed,
Dr. Shyam's
gentle
and
commanding
authority
was clear
for all to see.

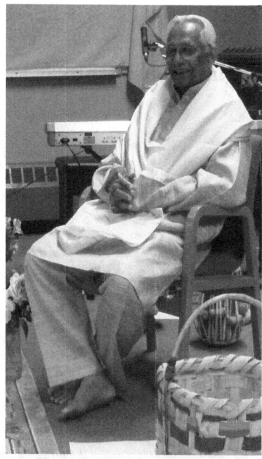

Figure 33

Right Relationship as Part of Right Behavior - Achara

The real function of relationship leads to the flowering of
humane humanity in each and every human being,
within the profound silence of the Immeasurable.

Women have influence, but men have the power to suppress. Man and woman
come from one seed. A chariot cannot move with one wheel.

The domain of love is expansion, eternity, all pervading capacity.
The light of love is simplicity.
Falling in love is easy. Being desperate is where there is no Spirit.
Rising in love is difficult. One who has risen is happy.

You are not an external body but an internal immensity, which is interconnected to the
whole cosmic created energy. You are connected to everything that has been created.

Increase your caliber of understanding. We have an inbuilt code, an operating manual. How
to decode it is the moral caliber of a person. Animals know where they reside. They have this
inbuilt decoding sensor. Human beings block everything because of selfish ends, fighting for
land, women, and gold. Knowing what "I am" and what "I am not" approaches Universal
Brotherhood. Then behavior and approaches to human problems become Universal.
You arrive at your full potential.

Deception is a perversion and its reception is a conversion leading to an inarticulate
conception. All such conceptions are inarticulate if they percolate.

Interactions must be natural, effortless, not contrived or enforced.
A ray of light is better than total darkness.

You must know the extent of your understanding and progress. Then you
can certify yourself as a Universal being, by yourself to yourself.

Despondency comes from trying to love someone else by abandoning oneself.

If you try to define a person, you defile them.
Bliss is timeless. Love is modification. We manifest Love by the right blending.
With the human mind, relationships don't relate. Usually, relationship is an attitudinal
fixation between people. Relationship is an apprenticeship where we pay dues.

Only the mind of God relates to everything. Genetically we are coded to all the great souls.
How do you become great? By grating yourselves.

God's love has a reciprocal duality.

What Is Desire?

Intension, Inner Tension, Desire, Longing

Scripture says that desire is not bad, but rather that desire should not become greed. Power corrupts, and power breeds greed. You have little things that you enjoy in your life. The whole creation is for your enjoyment. Real enjoyment has a ring without a wrong note. The *Vedas* never advocated refusing enjoyment but rather not to get attached to it. It is inhuman not to have desire. You are not a human being if you are without desires. But satisfaction is a myth, a diversion. Things looking a certain way are not what they are. Scriptures never mention that you should not have sex. They say to follow *Brahmacharya* to a certain extent in life until you acquire knowledge and have a control over your senses. To practice celibacy, in this sense, is to live in the consciousness of God, of the Creator. You have a vast expansion of your mind, which encircles the whole of creation. That beauty is one with the pure sexuality. That is the same resonance. Pure sexuality is not abusing sexuality, but it is upholding it to such a height that you become one with that. It is not the external sexuality. You become one with that then you enjoy the bliss of being in resonance with the opposite sex. Transformation should come on an individual basis. Every individual becomes part of an entire society, forming a bouquet. Different flowers are there, a whole variety, but they should form a bouquet.

*The real function of
relationship leads to the
flowering of humane
humanity in each and every
human being, within the
profound
silence of the
Immeasurable. Life
attracts life in a sense.
When we are
connected to life,
we must understand
life also,
and then we will
understand each other.
Understanding the
connectedness of life
requires that we
understand it
not just in one sense,
but in every way.*

*The ancient people,
without all these modern
instruments and scientific
experiments, said life is
everywhere, that the
whole creation is nothing
but life, including the
galaxies and stars,
planets, sun, and moon.
Everything has life.
Saint Francis said
Brother Sun and
Sister Moon.
He felt that
connectedness of life.*

Figure 34

On Love (A Cascade of Quotes)

What is love? That love you can never talk about. You do not know how deep it is, how vast. That great love came with the Immaculate Conception.

You cannot define love to its full extent. Love is all-pervading and all-evading.

Love is the driving force of consciousness that is caught in the life current without getting caught up. It is the essential factor of life that is luminous, never diminishing; [it is] an eternal sun that never sets.

Right relationships come if there is a connection through faith, sincerity, and truthfulness. The brain connections develop, and then the brain is a universal brain.

When love becomes a wart then it becomes a romantic fantasy. A wart comes where we have blocked the mind. St. John ate locusts to get rid of mental warts! (St. John's Wort). To get rid of mental warts, follow the universal law. It stops fickle mindedness.

Romance has become a Roman dance, a roaming antic, pining after something that makes us old and that becomes old also. Young people want to romance with the opposite sex, getting hurt three or four times and still not understanding what happened, committing the same blunder that renders asunder. Then there is repentance. Marriage can be a nine day's wonder and lifelong blunder. The world is full of stimulation. The modern world is all appearances. The world accepted all the falsehoods from different sources. People must admit when they are wrong. In the heart of hearts, they know they have committed a great blunder by succumbing to the deadliest weakness.

We look for antidotes but get into all this trouble by doting.

A heart wart comes when the intellect thinks it can overwhelm anything. The heart is the seat of God. It must be alert with awareness. There is adjacent awareness and distant awareness. Confusion comes with the reluctance to follow a spiritual course and establish oneself in the light of God, irrespective of all the things we do in the world.

Most relationships have a terrible ego on one side and a terrible submission on the other. A husband and wife need a leash. Virtue is the leash. Absolute knowledge puts on this leash. Existence, knowledge, and bliss are *Sat, Chit, Ananda. Ananda Aditya* is the maximum bliss accumulated.

No one should be under the control of a terrible ego.

Joy or *Ananda* in human awareness is the sense of aliveness, being in movement and breath.

Our love is provisional and perversion-al. We become very subtle. We have to develop gratitude and peace with no perversion. Service to the human race allows the right qualities to come out by reducing the negative. Be on the lookout; be vigilant for your defects.

If you love one person more than another, you try to correct yourself, but it is a second hand love. Equal love is an ideal. Do you love yourself? You love yourself as someone else's self. In spite of all those things we cannot love. One person you love in many ways. You do not have that one-pointedness. Then you deliberate and become a house of horror. In what way are you going to improve yourself? You have to balance your clarity and crudity, credibility and vulnerability, your ability and debility. You must be all sided. If you try to hit the nail on the head without practice, you hit your hand. When you hit the nail on the head, it is wonderful and "genderful."

Our birthright is to balance ourselves.

Love comes when you are being helped by the Divine grace. You have to make a right commitment, a willing participation in the Higher Self. You must be useful to yourself.

When we think vertically, we have a glimpse of that Divine glow.

When we put a seed of anger in the beautiful heart of God, then we have heart problems. Anger can destroy thousands of cells in the heart. Discrimination frees us from evil seeds in the mind. The heart is the seat of life. All senses merge into it. We pollute it and become pig hearted. We put money into a piggy bank and then are suffocated by that! We go on repeating actions of anger, jealousy, and hatred, and [we] love proportionally less.

Love with truth can breed hatred. If you are straightforward and truthful you can create enemies. I have a shield that kickbacks to the enemies. If you are straightforward, you don't fall into manipulations with others. If you don't follow straightforwardness, you become shallower. Then you have to wallow in telling falsehoods to your friends. Do not relegate the truth. Only God is your real friend. Solitude of soul is a sole attitude.

Those who shield you from truth and reality are your real enemies. Everything leads you to One Truth. People fail to utter truth and hide truth under falsehood. To tell falsehood is cowardice, an abominable ego.

Woman has a heart that knows everything. Man has knowledge that knows everything. To know the heart is to emancipate the ego.

To be shallow is to rely on a mode of behavior. The mode depends upon all the external articles because there is no article of faith.

Dependency brings failure and misery. We depend upon a material reality. Materialism is not bad, but the indulgence is. A moment of pleasure can bring a life of misery.

Depend upon your own integrity. Integrity is internal gravity.

Telling the truth is not just to burst out with conflicting ideas.

Conflict starts with conning (to con). There is deliberate competition and assertion of "my right." What is that right? It is a redundant show and indulgent action of force.

You can hear a thought, which is a cellular provocation and subatomic vibration.

Goodness has a tempered value. What we think is good for one person is not for another. Sometimes though, even if cruel, a surgeon's knife turns into something good.

The best way to apply right knowledge is to open up your heart and teach each other how to live a cooperative, graceful life, and how to respect others with great love and aptitude. To know a person is to know what they should do to enhance themselves, not to encourage in them the wrong things. Knowledge is a medicine of love. Righteousness, compassion, lack of enmity, lack of jealousy and hatred: these are the permanent medicines.

Existence is to prepare for non-existence. You see it most clearly in your pets. It is a revolving evolution and goes on revolving until it produces the essence, your essentiality of life.

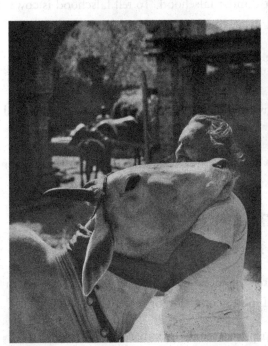

Figure 35

You are not an external body but an internal immensity
which is interconnected to the whole cosmic created energy. You are connected to
everything that has been created. Bliss is timeless. Love is modification.
We manifest Love by the right blending.

Figure 36

Guidance is to surrender one's impurities to the Divine. You have confidence in something higher than your identity. Romeo said to Juliet, "You're always in my heart." This confidence comes from knowing "the whole creation is in my heart." It is so vast that it contains the whole creation, including you. This heart is so vast; it is the ocean of love. This is the noble way of surrender.

Humane humanity means humility. It is the same root.

The light of faith is God in the person who enters the threshold of the immeasurable. You stand on the platform of humanity, and from there you take off.

To have a simple life is to prolong the life giving forces. With the absence of conceit, there is nectar inside. Make use of your own potentials and resources, not becoming resentful, gossiping and complaining. Gossip does not make a person spiritual. A blaming attitude is scandal mongering. But devotion can dissolve all this negativity.

Where your heart is, there your treasure is also. No one can take this away from you.

Bring your own resources into action. Protect and preserve the goodness. Have zeal to use the resources endowed by God, keeping that God inside you. Jesus said, "My voice is crying in the wilderness." The wilderness is the jungle of our mangled thoughts.

If there is a setback, do not worry about it; just go on doing one's duties. To surrender is to render service.

To study the mind and help others is as good as serving God. To serve the creation is serving God. Goodness is a spontaneous gift from oneself, from the Higher Principle.

We wrongly say a person is the "love of my life." It then becomes "the hate of my life." Such hate and love strangulate, the "templer strangler."

Love is not a passion. We must have a passion for love. When that is there, we think of what is really good for a person. When we follow that origin, of goodness, there is no conflict. The origin becomes a horizon, and we can expect a rainbow!

Two different things are love with respect and love without respect. Respect should go to deserving causes.

To have real heart is to see the seat of God everywhere. To be undivided is to not live on the surface of unreal assumptions. The task masters of division divide and rule. To love God is to love everybody because God is in everybody. To love the God in everybody means that God deserves that love. It is not to love one person only.

Love is the most dangerous thing. The whole world is after it. What is love? If it is the love of God, you must know God. One can never reach God, the unreachable, the un-possess-able. The vast expanse of oneself flows into the Godhead. Love and devotion are not a process. When we try to apply it, we get caught up in the process. The love of God can only come through grace.

Temples have low doorways so we can drop our egotism. When you take a bow, you don't growl.

Love is the thing that makes a person bend down and kiss the ground. God created the world out of love. It wasn't a fleeting, pornographic love but a piercing love. The soul of love is a human being.

Throughout his life span,
Dr. Shyam included all
creatures great and small
into his universal family.

Figure 37

Holiness of the Libido

The human race is above what we think. The human is the refracted light of God. *Maya,* or the veil of creation, is the reflection of God face to face. *Maya* (illusion) is also fruitful ignorance in that it is self-limiting. It has the purpose of drawing a veil over creation and in bestowing focalizing power and consciousness into individual manifestation. The human spectrum of loyalty to the Divine understands the holiness of the libido. The libido is the reservoir of instinctual energy. It is the driving force behind all human action and psychic energy. The light and breath of the Divine is refracted like light through a prism. The holiness of the libido is the pleasure principle of attraction to God. That is the Divine purpose of bliss. This libido is the *Kundalini,* rooted in the *Muladhara* chakra. The *Kunda* is the pit at the base of the spinal cord where the serpent power resides in three coils. When we give it a push through the breath, it rises through the central channel, the *Shushumna.* Knowing how to raise this energy, then we are not lost in the dungeon of the world. The energy is pushed upward and goes to the brain where the mind is illuminated. When the *Kundalini* energy rises in the central *Shushumna* channel, then the brain is universal. It belongs to everyone, and whoever comes near will be changed.

The bliss principle in the *Kundalini* is sublimated to the God principle. It is the passion of creation. *Kundalini* raised has different functions:

1. Love
2. Refinement
3. Restoration

A physical relationship is not about fulfillment but enrichment. The infantile nature becomes obsolete. Growth is connected to nature, but it becomes fixated and arrested. The culture is in the infant stage. There is an infantile attachment to the genitals. Flirting saps energy. We can lose this bliss by having sex under the wrong circumstances. Is there an opposite sex or an opposing sex? Circumstances provide fertile ground for going astray. Even a thief knows he is harming a person.

Extraneous commonalities lead to defeat. When you go according to the culture, you always meet with vultures!

If the *Muladhara* chakra is not active, the sex drive becomes active. Sex only gives a sense of relief by the release of instinctual energy. Masturbation dissipates potency. Sex can be a dependency and a fix. It is meant to be creatively procreative. We give sex a chance but not our life. Be independent.

When a child is born, there is a separation between the parents, and there can be a surge of hormonal iniquity. The girl manipulates the father, and the boy the mother. This is a manipulation of the genetic code. If they want to correct God, they go totally wrong. This split in the human psyche causes fragmentation and is where our ideas of sin come from. Forty thousand years ago humanity took a wrong turn.

Everybody is affected by their own ignorance. Too much excitement takes you out of yourself. It affects the rest of your life. Excitement is the titillation of the senses in the field of *Maya.* Arrest yourself from these follies. Experience can bring joy but can also turn into your enemy. By drawing energy out, it makes us weaker. Materialist applications of energy aggrandize the ego for egotistic, selfish, demoralizing purposes. So called religious people can misuse energy to bamboozle others. A vulnerable person succumbs to temptation, attraction and repulsion. Even the Tantriks and Sheiks spoiled *Kundalini Yoga*. When it is used only for sexual activities, then the person loses energy and becomes weak, falling into the afflictions of the mind: lust, anger, pride, self-intoxication, covetousness, and jealousy. Although lust is necessary to have children, we fall a prey to the instinctual energy by getting an "itch," which affects the genital area of the brain. Men think it is their "right" to enjoy a woman, and the ego occupies the mind. The Divine qualification for lasting bliss is lost. A person can become almost mad. The brain is deprived of its status when the mind creates a fall in the stature of this energy. All commit mistakes when we come from a series we call our life and are not strong enough to hold the virtue. Virtue becomes an enemy and a target. Experience never helped us to be grounded. We need our hands to be folded to be grounded. Anything we think is easy to grab is injurious. When the energy is brought down to the lowest human level, it leads to the deprivation of longings without belonging. Disease comes, dis-ease, and will haunt us. Do not think your brain is taciturn or useless. Each cell of your brain is active in billions of universes. It is so vast. We make ourselves so tiny.

The libidinal energy is the sacred energy from the psyche in its prime of performance. It can give the status of immortality, and this energy must be used for a good purpose; otherwise it turns on us. The mind should roll over on itself, and in the seventh fold it becomes the Divine Apotheosis. The folds conserve the energy so it doesn't leak out. Then the mind will be mind in the last stage of transformation.

In the raising of the libidinal *Kundalini* energy, we do not become mad but blissful and loveable. It can come as a sudden upsurge that purifies energy and then we are fully content in the Self. Other things become redundant. The danger comes from *Mahda*, when the ego rises as well and we do not distinguish. With contentment rather than the intoxicated craving of the ego, we tread the path to the Godhead.

At a later stage in life (after the productive and generative stages), yoga also gives us ways to raise, amplify this energy, and it rises like mercury. Yoga yokes to the Creation and all of life. The Lord and Goddess (*Shiva and Shakti*) become one internally. The person's serpent power joins to the Divine Self. In the *Tantra Shastra*, the human is enjoined to romance with the deity. In this sublimation, the person mates with the Divine principle, where at that stage one is not distracted by the male or female partner. The energy rises to the point of absorption in Bliss or *Ananda*. This intuitive energy is an intracellular energy and will not shake. Once we raise this power and it permeates the cells, it makes us effulgent and above the bickering of the world. We then are one with the ancient *Rishis*. The *Rishis* are in between all the kinds of beings, gods, demons and humans. They maintain the order of the Supreme Law. They control the world, and creation is engineered through them by the Divine Bliss of God. *Guru* means light giver. The wondrous act of the heart makes the world happy, not locked in the brain's syndromes. Your old self will be swept away.

Devotion is not a feeling. It is the highest love. Devotion is real absorption. Then this love will correct us if we go wrong. We become selfless from this *Ananda* when it stops at the throat chakra. Beyond the throat, we go to the *Paramatman* the origin of oceanic bliss experienced by all newborn babies. Here we do not think of the psyche at all because we are all-consciousness.

Libido is generally psycho-anal sexual energy from the psyche itself in its prime of performance. The libido can liberate or trap. It can lift to the spiritual and give us so much energy and strength to function in the world, even if the world turns against us. Some Sufis understood this but if this process is not done properly, there is still attraction to this miserable world. To control this energy and use it for energetic purposes brings reconciliation between the human being and the psyche. Celibacy is contemplation and concentration on God all the time, and then you celebrate... Always live in God.

Life is precious. Do not waste it on puny things. Do not make it into a puny something. Without essence, there is no life. Without the essential, you cannot work. You must know how to preserve the potency. The one Reality is potent, but the world becomes impotent. Every human activity has selfishness. Man gives but grudges the giving. God is not selfish but giving. Creation has the internality of the creative energy. Learn your life with patience, how to give joy, how to handle a thorn. Your actions are thorny when you are horny! The problem is lack of reverence. Help the body maintain its ease and healthiness.

*The psychic aspect of a human being is
humanity. The letting go of this is
the weakness. With humanity, you
become transparent and not opaque.
With transparency, the transference of
material input comes to you,
when you are tuned with your
Self and the knowledge of what
you want to know.*

Figure 38

Only Love Can Free

The majority of families are dysfunctional. Most often, these are patriarchal families where the power is used excessively without any kind of discrimination. The family strictly follows a set pattern and is indoctrinated by one aspect of life. Therapists often come from dysfunctional families, whether they were abusive or had other problems. When we in our ordinary minds give to others, there is usually motivation. So the love is rooted in a fear that has selfishness also. When you are expecting or anticipating love from somebody, that love is conditional. When you have motivation behind it, there is selfishness. That means you are expecting love, therefore hesitating to love. That is what happens in marriage. People are conditioned by their past, so it is like the relationship is frozen in the past, in the patterns, petrified. Two petrified people say, "I do." Like the drive up windows in Las Vegas, they go to one window to get the marriage certificate and go around to the other side to get the divorce certificate. This is our system. People live their conditions and not their lives. There is no real love in that. People may fantasize about love, but that is fantastic love. Those ideals are fads in the mind, figments of our imagination. We have glorified the dysfunctional.

I think the duty of therapists is to free the patient from the therapist! But nowadays, there's a kind of conspiracy to keep the patient, and that becomes dysfunctional therapy. The therapist is supposed to have a big love for the patient. If that love is not there, the [therapist] cannot free up that person. Love frees and not anything else. Only love can free from everything. Love always stands against bondage. And friendship is the same thing. It always stands against bondage. In good friendship, there is no binding. You do not become a slave to your friends or them to you. Love never makes a person a slave. Authority might make a person a slave, but in love there is no authority. In nature there is no reward or punishment but only consequences. Love is so humble, like the ocean, very powerful but still humble. The whole creation is nothing but love.

Satsang Talk, February, 1995

Compassion

All human beings need to have a fulfilling, common goal. In my opinion, this goal would be to grow in the all-embracing awareness of compassion and to maintain a passion for harmony with a canorously empathic disposition. This is a sure way to overcome human frailties, failures, and pitiful trepidation.

Compassion is not just a psychological expression nor a mere passion, but it is an eventful phenomena in the primordial psyche. It was Dante who said, "Compassion is not a passion, but a noble disposition of the soul, made ready to receive love, mercy, and other ennobling passions."

Lack of compassion may lead to carnal passion and desire to possess, to own, and to get obsessed with material possessions. It is said that the primal psyche emerged with creation itself, and it is aptly a concomitant of the split in the unity [that] existed before creation. The split was appropriate and necessary for the eventful diversification of creation.

In the course of evolution, the primal psyche branched out in each and every created entity having life, thought, feelings, and movement. As individuals grew in the process of evolution, he or she created many arbitrary divisions and identified with those divisions as distinctive individual ability-forming propensities. Now I may allude to the original split as a compassionate act on the part of the combined forces of creation involved in each other as male and female, yin and yang, or *Prakriti* and *Purusha*. Apparently, there is a difference in the density of these two forces. In the condensation process, they became distinctly separate, but they remain attracted to each other by the gravitational force of love and passion. In the human world, when love and passion combine serenely and purposefully with the effacement of self-interest, it becomes compassion. This compassion is therefore inbuilt in the individual psyche, but becomes a victim of the prevalent and active as a functional aspect of individuality and individuation. This brings about identity crises leading to a crisis of consciousness. Psychologically, this aspect is considered necessary for the purpose of the growth and actualization of capabilities and possibilities inherent in the growing psyche or expanding consciousness. If this process gets multiplied or involved in the ego centeredness, it becomes a motivational force for ill-conceived and hierarchical superiority and depth instability. The ego which rises through the split in its field of activities tends to carve cleavages of conflicting personality traits and produces annoying cleavers. The ego's tendency is to identify with splits and separateness. This seemingly anomalous attitudinal disorder leads to psychological problems and the abbreviation of the intent intrinsically inherent in the primal psyche. This may lead to wrong doings, wrong thinking, and wrong actions.

Isolation plays an important part in the factor-fact complex. Here, compassion is subjugated and relegated to almost a state of non-existence. All the important scriptures of the world proclaim that compassion is a stepping stone to any spiritual adventure. Compassion is closely associated with the spirit, and an absence of compassion leads to a distortion of the functions of the spirit. This may be the main cause of modern day conflict in the individual and collectively in the society as a whole. The society is built by individuals as partners in a process of socialization and functional family orders with differences and derivatives. As the conflicting trends infiltrate deeply into the elements of the psyche, it generates waves of fear and insecurity. With this seemingly defensive front projected, it withdraws into inaction and blocks the path to harmony, love, and the valuable assets of coordination and integration. The integral substance becomes a mere shadow, and this shadow not only follows the individual but overcasts the knowing and understanding faculty.

Mindful people, whom we call sages, or custodians of ancient wisdom, have valuable things to say about the human goals and the paths leading to these goals. These paths are beset with vicissitudes and painful turns and twists. As the multiple splits go on increasing, the psyche, which is the repository of love and compassion, fragments and splinters. Each fragment has a viable record of failures and deficient performances. The process involved replicates the existence of ignorance even in the solutions tried by different aspects of psychology and psychiatry. As has been stated elsewhere, the original split in the unity was integral to the creative harmony. As such, unity becomes integral in the process of the evolution of the created. It is evident that there is a problem in the process of growth. The problem is this fragmentation. To make the psyche whole is the purpose of psychology and psychiatry. The origin of neurosis and psychosis has not been rightly understood in relationship with the primal split. This failure, construed as success, allows the accumulation of pieces and fragments of disturbance in the spectrum of the psyche constituted by the eccentricities of ego-centeredness. Remedial measures based on misunderstanding or no understanding of the cause and effect of the original split are responsible for a series of failures in tackling the psychological problems and the emotional upheavals in a large section of the human race.

Only with sensitivity can human beings become compassionate, not with sensationalism, which is connected to the sensual world. Sensationalism renders people barbaric. Human beings made a blunder. Heaven is all sensitivity.

It is therefore necessary for knowledgeable counselors and therapists to go deep into the alternate healing techniques based on compassion, love, and wisdom. The elixir of life is at hand, but one should know how to use it. It is therefore necessary to investigate the possible aspect of the ancient theory of rebuilding the psyche with the wholeness of spirit and spirituality. Compassion is a total force. It can unite all the splits and make the psyche whole. Compassion includes the sacrificial serenity and self-effacing grace of inner immensity. The Divine always revels in compassion and reveals the mystery of life in love, which is the only panacea for all the ills and odds. Life is an eternal glorification of the Divine in the finite, and the finite is the grateful womb of grace and creation of the Divine as its eternal birthright.

Newsletter Essay, 1997

Chapter VIII

HEALING

Godliness is remembering the holiness of your Self.

In God's kingdom there is no darkness, only delay.

The ancients believed that God writes on your forehead: your Karma *(actions and consequences), your* Dharma *(lawful action), and your* Varma *(shield).*
You don't read it but you realize it.

That Divine Will illuminates your life, and wrong actions can be detected in no time.
But it can become dim and dark through encrustation.
Everyone who advises others should practice first.
Truthfulness reverses the cycle of suffering.

There is no end of anything.
Evil doers have strong wills. The ending of evil occurs but a trace
remains and comes back when a being is welcoming of it.

Vasanas (positive or negative traces, tendencies) can be reawakened.

In the Pralhadha *(reabsorption of the universe or the deluge),*
the Atman *(Divine Self) is not completely gone. That "I" has to be there for creation.*

That is the "I," or the "EYE."
Eternally Your Entertainment!

The Atman *(Divine Self within) is* Brahman *(the unfathomable universal totality).*

Console others from the bottom of your heart to help them amend
their ways. This is a continuous flow of love.

And DNA is Divine Nature in Action!

If children are good, the Father takes care of them. Every cell in our body sings His Name. The cells always remember the Source of their abundance. This is the difference between you and your cells. Do you want a cell life or a stale life? Your behavior shows how God relates to you.

Right thinking (Vichara) comes out of your right behavior.
Behavior creates thought, which affects all your cells.
When the mind is a problem, the body is at random.

*Nature's kindness and innate knowledge of all life
essences meet in the human being in a torrent.*

*There are two movements on the
path of human life, the
movement of outgoing or the
movement of incoming or returning;
the involutionary path and the
evolutionary path. The deeoer you
get involved in matter, the deeper is
the illusion and ignorance.
The evolution to Spirit leads to the
essential and true nature,
which is inherent in us.*

Figure 39

111

Question: Can Suffering Be Habitual? (A Cascade of Quotes)

It's a habit. You want to entangle yourself in something. The spider weaves a web from its own material. It knows where to stay and how to pull the one string when some insect comes. The spider never gets caught up in his own web… but human beings weave webs and get caught in them. So, who is intelligent? A spider or human being?

Beware of your inclinations, delusions, capacities, aptitudes, and attitudes. Beware of false teachers and avoid occult inclinations. Don't fall into the intoxication of psychic phenomena.

Everything is a teacher, from a fox to a hoax.

Anxiety can come from a collective falsehood. A conference can be a con-inference! Partiality is a falsehood. People make rejection a custom. There is an unspoken agreement because everyone wants to be popular.

Dishonesty comes with wealth, but the earth can support all people.

Faith is nothing but the participation in the dynamic action of reality in reality, and it is about reality. You don't talk about suffering, you talk to suffering. That's the beauty of it. You talk to suffering. Can you talk to suffering? Tell yourself when you are angry or jealous that you are and should not be. Jealousy blocks the incoming goodness. Ask, "Why should I listen to the diabolical ego?" Drive away your ignorance. Methods do not work unless you have truth. Be so bold and courageous and talk to suffering. There lays the key to get rid of suffering. At that moment, when you talk to suffering, the Divine intervenes. We need an intercession in our intricate situations. And He takes away your suffering.

Patients do not get better often because they do not tell the truth to their doctors. They lose their humanity, but it is the nature of the human being to tell the truth and bear the bitter consequences.

The Kingdom of God is within you; your temple is the kingdom. It's always there. You only have to have the understanding to realize that's the kingdom of God. It's your own kingdom. It's not something different. It's your own kingdom. God is not a miserly fellow. "That guy God" is God. He will not build a kingdom for Himself. He has built it for you. He holds this kingdom and every kind of blessing on a silver platter. But we are so puny, so tiny; we don't even think that we deserve that kingdom.

We shy away from it. He invites you all the time.

The logic behind psychotherapy is a spiritual awareness of the connection to the totality of life. The gist is leading a person to spirituality. Anywhere else is pathetic and pathological.

Spirituality gives the gist of all that is life, a state of joy in the Ultimate God.

The all is nothing but the 'I,' which is present in everything.

There is truth in ancient practices. Supplicants would walk on their knees to the *Sanctum Sanctorum* of the temple. Exercises in prayer are meant to help the body attain a stature and heal.

We have a life of show not substance. It is so important to give up falsehood. Surrender creates health. When you really pray, you don't prey on others.

Faith cures. Faith is the real healer, OK? But you must have that goal. Don't be victims of habits and the psycho-sensorial automatisms. With real faith, the heart, mind, and body are in the right place. Otherwise someone is there to censor you. You cannot sit in a place and contemplate faith in the name of meditation. You must have the dynamic activity of action. Then you'll be consumed and your life will be effulgent, full of prayer. Your life will be the Abode of God, that's actually the Void; the *Sanctum Sanctorum*. But full. Full of activity.

*Yoga means
to yoke yourself to goodness,
yoke yourself to God.
Yoga makes a body ready
to receive higher vibrations
like a musical instrument, and
it becomes more sensitive.
What note the body sings
depends upon what tension
exists in the vehicle.*

*God is weightless. [When giving
yourself to God]
going up is easier and
easier—you become lighter.*

*Aim high, according to your
potential. Potentiality is
goodness:
Richness of thought,
Amicability,
Thoughtfulness,
Coordination.*

*Resistance to going up is ego.
Lassitude with clinging, anger,
desire, greed—
weighs you down. These are
intrinsic in life activities,
but an excess of the above
comes from ignorance.
Attachment is fear.*

*To accumulate in life is OK, but
don't be attached to it.
If you are attached,
you will suffer a lot.*

Figure 40

114

On Nature (A Cascade of Quotes)

To Go Far Away from Nature is to be Nearer to Anarchy

Nature's kindness and innate knowledge of all life essences meet in the human being in a torrent. Negative tendencies are acquired. Positive qualities are natural.

Our own nature is correlated with the outside nature. It also has cruelty and love. Cruelty is also good in that it teaches you great endurance and tolerance.

Nature produces nectar and poison. They are actually balanced. Poison even helps plants to grow.

Sometimes plants need a pat and sometimes they need a slap, as do people.

Why does sickness come to us? It comes to remind us of our mortality. Your pride is gone, and it [sickness] topples down. Pride and prejudice go together.

There is an ultimate coordination between good and evil. Sages face the problems and take them on, remaining compassionate. All problems are external. When you internalize the whole thing, it cramps in the mind.

All the organs do not question but go on doing their prescribed work. Each cell in the body has particular duties. We do nonsense to our organs and make them fail because we think we know. All facilities in our body are there to facilitate your functions. If you overdo, organs become useless. Everything is limited. Cells are connected to the universal spectrum. The world has already heard these things but doesn't pay attention. It is always in tension.

Voice and sound travel in space. All your organs produce a beautiful sound. Each individual has a sound note, a sole property, and an intense aspiration. The sole aim of life is to be the soul, individual solidarity. When you know the soul, mystery becomes the sole property. You must fit your lifestyle into this intention, intensity without tension, and be emancipated. The mind of God is the enormous mind of the human being.

Even though the body is bound to deteriorate because it has to go back to the origin of bliss, and we have to discard this body; if we abuse the body with cranky ideas, then we go to the wrong place, "hell." The deeds we have done are not buried but have a life of their own. They become more rejuvenated. Therefore it is so important to do good, not according to theology or some ideas, but just go on "doing good and being good."

All things are created by that intelligence which is not tangible, which has given rise to all mysterious things that the intellect cannot comprehend. The healer is beyond all those things. The healer is not intellect, but the healer is embedded in the primordial intelligence that has created all.

Figure 41

116

On Healing (A Cascade of Quotes)

We have such a great immune system when we concentrate on the Self and think of the great power that has given you power. Fight, stand, and face every situation in calmness, and it will go back to that person. Your *dharma* is not to run away.

The power of the soul gives luster and immunity. Beauty is in the soul power. If the soul is lost, then everything is lost. The soul is a pole. A lack of luster comes from chronic fear. There can be benign or malignant fears.

In a way the whole human body is a disease of the soul. The highest principle cannot be undertaken in the world. It is not achieved as long as the soul inhabits the body.

The *dharma* is the adamantine justice that coordinates all elements by the one principle of truth, faith, and reverence. At the command of *dharma*, all cosmic energies are harnessed.

Medicines are different in each country. Natural factors make for different potencies. When you diagnose a person, you must know the origin of that person. Monkeys found quinine!

Even boredom can be ecstasy and inspiration. With boredom can come psychic amelioration, but we try to erase people's boredom. People do not know how to be content.

The test of contentment is mental equilibrium. Yoga is equanimity, the balance of body, heart and mind. Yoga inhibits the mind's outgoing faculties and running away from the truth. Everything is collected to one point of concentration.

When the heart, which is celestial, is not balanced, it oozes. The brain can be bamboozled, the mind contracts and spirit fades. Spirit is that which evaporates.

The equinox of the human being is to balance all those things. There is a mathematical tabulation through the universe. The purpose is to renew the Self.

Experiment on yourself. See what works. Advil is good for pain relief. "Add Will!"

Everything has a cure, but these may backfire. The problem of relapsing is not knowing how to relax.

We have a dispensary in the mind. It is a compounder as well.

Do not go in for energy work. If you get energy from someone else, it is a contaminated energy. Use your own energy, which is innately pure.

The psychology of transformation is to feel that unity inside and to understand nature. When you know how to read nature, your mind expands to cover everything. This is *Purushottama*, the Great Lord. Intuit into it.

At every stage, there is constitutional change. Even the blood changes every ten minutes. A main point in health is protecting your blood. If you cannot keep your blood pure, your heart is in jeopardy. Pure blood comes from pure thought.

Reflection comes because of affliction. We reflect because we want to be free of affliction. Reflection will bring awareness of deflections that keep the truth at bay and off on a tangent, bringing corruption. If we go to the root of a problem, then it can be routed.

Roots are the support system, helping us to adapt to the environment. But we adopt an attitude of the ego without gratitude, and then we have no latitude. We live in a sequential life but adopt deflections [that] the intellect plays a part in choosing. We play a part on the stage of life, but only the cosmic context sees the whole panorama.

Intelligence is a choiceless affirmative movement in consciousness. Life is an affirmation. It is not "I am living," but life itself asserts.

Divine intoxication gives a polarity and impetus to complacency. Discontent is built into creation.

To affirm is not to go on repeating affirmative adjuncts, which reflect our own misunderstandings. It is to be connected to all of life. Our consciousness is as a small part floating in an ocean of awareness of the tremendous flow of life.

Concentration expands itself into the metaphysical expanse. One point is infinitesimal. The mind (*ekarchitta*) can be at one point [that] doesn't move, but it expands and contracts. You are the expansion to cover the whole creation, including the Creator.

This world is a holy land. You can enjoy or suffer. The whole of space is there to go anywhere you want, but you have to find that capacity, power, and energy to go, to travel.

A permanent truth is descending. Everyone can change. The truth can never change. The Divine can never change.

Healing takes people to the Source. If you take them to the Source, they will not be sore. They will soar higher!

Sages practiced penance for years and years, but they didn't dwell on God, they dwelled on themselves—and dragged God to them!

In ancient times, religion, faith, and spirituality lived in the great seers. Wherever life existed, life itself whispered all these understandings into space. This is what we call the inner voice...or the voice of God. So life itself whispered all those things into space or the ear of space. That is how it comes to us. In Sanskrit this is called "Atashiwa," that which comes from the voice of the sky, the voice of creation. So life whispered how we are to live life. This came to us by tradition, before writing. And the tradition was oral, it was not written. Creation started with a sound, one syllable, expanded into so many things. Sound has the power to create the entire universe.

Figure 42

On Healing: Darkness and Light

Is the darkness the absence of light, or does it have a separate existence? Or is it an entity by itself? To my mind, darkness is just the absence of light. When there is no light, there is darkness. In the Bible, it is said, "In the beginning, let there be light." Indian scriptures say in the beginning there was light, which came from an interchange between the female energy and the male energy. These existed in the totality of existence itself. And then that friction caused the tremendous explosion of the big bang, exploding into millions of globules, which became many universes. The forces of attraction and repulsion are inherent in nature as primordial principles in material creation. These forces unite and operate as unconditional love on a cosmic level. In the world, they are forces of reaction and retroaction. In the human mind, they operate as forces of love and hatred. The entire thought process is governed by the divisive influence of these forces. They are beneficial if they are understood in the light of reason and virtue. They help to discriminate right from wrong. They manage to keep the universal laws operating without disruption among the heavenly bodies and their relationships. This means that even the planets have attraction and repulsion. They stand at a particular distance. These principles promote awareness, interconnectedness, and harmony. So the real healing is not about drugs, or medicine, but about bringing more life force, more energy into the living being.

All scriptures say that life is God given and a holy thing. If these laws are not understood, they have a devastating effect upon the vital functions of life. They may lead to violence, jealousy, hatred, tyranny, ingenious manipulations, and exploitations. Enslaved by ignorance, the human mind may become a playground for good and evil. It becomes possessive, and envious. So many evil thoughts enter into the field of perceptions such as, "You and I; mine and yours; my religion is better than your religion; my country is better than your country," and so on. What happens to life when darkness comes? What happens to the light when it is obscured by ignorance? There are a million folds of ignorance. If you observe the world, you will notice that these things are going on in every nation. There is turmoil in the world because of the lack of understanding of the human qualities inherent in the primordial principles. We are swayed by appearances. If the human being who can understand and go beyond all these conditions, however tempting they appear to be, the person can go beyond this vicious thought process. When the forces of attraction and repulsion are united, they operate as serenity, just serenity.

When thought becomes corrupted, actions become corrupted. Do you go to the source of your thoughts? Good and evil exist in thought and not in the Ultimate Reality. As long as our actions are dictated by a negative thought process, we are bound to have wars, destructions, and calamities. The moment we understand the mechanism of thought, we transcend it. If we are honest to ourselves, then we transform the entire process into benevolent processes. Thoughts are sounds we hear inwardly. If we think 'Jesus,' we hear 'Jesus.' If we think, 'flower,' we hear 'flower.' Since God is a good thought, every religion in the world tells us to think of God. Religion means "binding back". Going back to the origin of yourself means you don't get absorbed in that; [rather], it absorbs you. Religion is your faith and absorption in goodness. If we do not think a good thought, we fall into a negative and discordant sound pattern. We should not, therefore, allow our minds to chatter. We still the mind by the practice of meditation and by being totally attentive to life. Thought has substance, but please do not abuse the substance. Transform it, and use it as an end to all means that cause greed and destruction.

Through this body we serve everything that has been created: By planting trees you serve nature, by planting trees and watering them; you talk to people, you serve by talking; then you treat people, you serve by treating; and you serve yourself by eating, by thinking.

The diseases you call have come from the wants, not from the needs, but from the wants, so the wants have given rise to or breed the diseases. It is physiological, physical, mental, everything. Every want we have, and our wants are so great. We cannot cope with them and call them emotions. It is not possible to get what you want. You don't know what you need.

Emotions are nothing but produced by the wants; we cannot cope. We are slaves of the emotions; we are still slaves. We are in a condition of addiction. Toxins intoxicate. All the pharmacies are making money and killing people. We are not free; we are slaves to all the diseases, slaves to all kinds of shortcomings and upheavals. Emotions are intangible, yet they have a powerful influence.

So if the emotions are not in motion, if they are stagnant, that's how the problem comes. If they are just flowing like the river, then there won't be any problem. That person says this body is mine, are you working on that very body or that which says "the body is mine." [Students reply: "You're working on that which says the body is mine."] Right, when you realize that you are ready.

The life process has a mathematical[ly] precise formula. Our life, though, is a rendition of what is holy, healthy and wholesome. You must carry exactly what you need, and that comes when you're integrated. When you realize this, "I" is not this body. Why you have got a body is nature's great gift to experience, to experience yourself as the creation. Not as so and so. Only the human body can experience it, so the human body is so important; it is just not five feet some inches and so many pounds. It is so immense. Consciously you have to experience certain things. That means, what happens is your consciousness has expanded to such an extent that it has covered everything. But, if you consciously experience all those things, that means you are experiencing the entire universe consciously, not unconsciously after death. Fear of death is fear of losing the bliss of the free flow of life. We hate death because we don't remember there is no death. Even after death, you don't experience death. The real intelligent expression of all those things is in your life. And when death comes there is a resurrection, and that is why so many people who have experienced out of body experiences have seen this light and splendor. In that sense we don't die. If you are integrated and embedded in that intelligence, there is always remembrance. Awareness is the surgeon, and the integral gravity remains. Awareness is not an attitude but an at-one-tude, attunement and atonement, at-one-ment.

This body is really meant to hold that consciousness, which will expand and envelop the entire creation, and will have that experience and enjoy it. Therefore life is a joy: Life is Joy. It comes from the eternal joy. Life is spread over everywhere – this whole thing is life. But, when you say "I live my life," you live your conditions, not life, just the conditions. We fight for the labels, we die for the labels.

So the main point I'm trying to say is the health of everybody, all of us, depends upon the harmony that we establish in our life, that is actually health, a gift. Grace is nothing but establishing harmony. If you establish harmony there is always grace upon you. That means you are graceful all the time.

When you do a massage you can read a lot of things from that, where the energy is stuck. The touch is very important; when you touch a body, that touch is where the exchange of energy takes place. And if you have great Love for the patient, the patient will be healed because it is Love that heals.

What is the meaning of healing? It comes from the same root: healing, holy, and healed. It is sacred. Whole and healed all come from the same root that means wholeness. To heal a person and to make one whole is the same meaning. And when you are whole you are holy, sacred. Wholeness is integration of body, mind, and the Spirit.

We have a total misunderstanding about ourselves, and a total mistaken identity of the whole human being. In the wholeness of the creation a human being is a separated entity by identification. We have identified with these five feet and some inches of body and external appearance, not internal functions. Therefore, we don't know a lot of things about ourselves. You are not an external body but an internal immensity, which is interconnected to the whole cosmic created energy. You are connected to everything that has been created.

To say "I know this and that" is the fragmentation of the personality. I have studied this. I have studied that or whatever. See that's the fragmentation of a healer. If you identify things as a Rolfer, you're not a healer. So don't identify. When you identify, you "indent," putting your teeth into it! What I mean is: as you identify with the body and appearance, you identify with the words and what they do. When a practitioner is conceited the patient actually treats the practitioner. That is not the total healing art. Any technique will help; it's not just the Rolfing that will help or acupuncture. Any technique will help if you are integrated. Any technique you use, will work, if you are integrated. If you say, "I have healed this person," you can't. That's the ego. That will block the healing process. Sometimes help simply helps the vices in a person. The healing is a spontaneous act, and even a healer doesn't know he has healed a person. One who perceives the wholeness of the creation can create wholeness in oneself.

What I'm trying to tell you is that there are things in you that can't be measured, that cannot be counted, and they are more important than the things you count and measure. And when you work on a person you are not just working on the bones and muscles, you are working on the whole person, and the whole person is immeasurable.

All things are created by that intelligence which is not tangible, which has given rise to all mysterious things [that] the intellect cannot comprehend. The healer is beyond all those things. The healer is not intellect, but the healer is embedded in the primordial intelligence that has created all those things.

It's not the technique that makes a healer, not the technology that makes a healer, but it is the essences behind all those things. If you know forty-eight herbs well, you can treat thousands of diseases. The essence is that, "I am the product of this intelligence that is whole always." That is why it cannot be unholy. It is always sacred, always holy, always whole. So you must know that a healer is that, nothing else.

Healing is an impartial, impersonal, spontaneous, Divine act that works through you – you are an instrument.

Satsang Talk, "Healing" 1997
(Editor's Note: Some of these paragraphs appear in Forces of Attraction and Repulsion)

Chapter IX

LIBERATION FROM THE NARROW EGO TOWARD SELF-REALIZATION

Vicious thinking is to say "because I can." Think before you take a step.
When you do, be very careful. Look twice before you leap. We live on the surface
of unreal assumptions. You seduce yourself and then reduce yourself.

People who never believe in the spiritual have their hearts in a stupor. The mind is
masquerading. They talk about false things and ruin their own and other's lives.
They suppress the truth and spread falsehood. This is the path of destruction.

The mind is like a rear view mirror. Objects appear closer than they are.
Accepting the mirror as correct is the human defect and illusion.

You give a meaning to your life, but that meaning is a misnomer. A real name is not commercial.

Confusion is a condition, an infusion of fragmentation.

The limit of ego is the fixated attachment to identity. A demonical ego has the hunger for power.

Only goodness gives life. The Divine dispensation is not a demonical compensation.

First be grounded. Have a strict, proper, unassailable conviction. Resolve is an
inspirational, uncalculated, integrated force that brings reconciliation.

A word is a powerful interaction between existence and non-existence.

Spirituality is utter sanity.

Revolving evolution goes on revolving until it produces the essence, the essentiality of life.

Realization is awareness of the totality of your Self connected to all of life. One is
all that is, was, and will be. The cipher is zero. Zero down on yourself.

When you are in tune with your real Self, you atone and attain. Do you fail yourself or follow yourself? You can bribe yourself to attain the status where you will not fail yourself. Failure is not the option of life. Success is the mainstay of life, not worldly success. You succeed when you transcend yourself. You'll be one with and in tune with the vibratory aspect of the whole of creation.

Figure 43

Cleansing the Negative Mind (A Cascade of Quotes)

To think one knows when one does not know is a dire disease.

Stupidity breeds cunningness.

The negative mind is an interchangeable imposition and becomes an imposter.

Why does one breed animosity unless one is weak and perverted? Drug abuse affects the brain, and then the person has a bone of contention with everyone. A bone of contention is not biodegradable. Weakness can be unlimited. Weakness is not caused by lack of energy but lack of understanding. The way is to stand under and rise above. Goodness is limited because it is concentrated and consecrated.

Insecurity, inferiority, and conceit are self-negation and mental dementia. They come from brooding, greedy habits, projection outside the Self, and recruiting oneself to do acts [that] should not be done. A projection is a moving image. Projection is a rejection of the real.

A greed exchange is thinking we have to exchange support for each other's egos. We succumb to ignorance and not intelligence. Ignorance welcomes ignorance.

The most difficult mindset to overcome is the mindset of convenience.

Feeling is a delusion.

Optimism is an optical illusion.

When a person is viciously bad they try to cause harm to others, creating chaos.

We cheat ourselves. We have complexes, depressive complexes, and don't mind our own business.

When we fall into the lowest human level, disease comes and the brain is deprived of its status. The brawn is gone, too. These are the "goners." Some are born into a tradition of hate and jealousy. Hate corrodes and occupies the whole system. We have prejudice against so many things. As long as you have prejudice, you will never learn. Animals do not have prejudice.

We try to exonerate ourselves from sin by false methods and therefore have so many diseases. People go to sages not to know the truth but to strengthen their belief, which doesn't work. To have a belief or a nonbelief in God is still belief.

The word is still there. God is the word. Truth is always truth. You know it inside yourself. This thing called truth and reality is not seen but felt: "I am alive, my pulses are throbbing, my heart is beating." Faith is the knowing you exist. Death is also a reality, but we have a wrong concept of illusion. Behind illusion is a truth.

We live on the surface of unreal assumptions.

How do you know God is there? How do you know you are there? People do not even know how they are born.

To rise above social influences cannot be done with imagination. Imagination goes on imagining, creating illusion and fantasy. Creative imagination is an inner fire, but sentimentality is fantasizing.

You seduce yourself and then reduce yourself.

The mind is like a rear view mirror. Objects appear closer than they are. Accepting the mirror as correct is the human defect and illusion.

The mind has a loitering habit with impudence and gullibility. When we hop here and there, like a frog, the snake comes to eat us! When we divide and fragment the self, and corrupt the mind, we can never say "I know." The idea of "I" is a knot in the human heart.

The false identity becomes angry, similar to when you have a fence around a compound. Anger is a reaction to something you don't like. There is turmoil of cells inside. Falsehood makes the cells tremble, causing a tremor. The physical upshot of inner turmoil is an earthquake. Marshal these cells, and take their help. The cells cannot be neutral because they work according to your reactions. The organs are intelligent. They follow universal law, not your law.

You give a meaning to your life, but that meaning is a misnomer. A real name is not commercial.

What gives meaning is the articulation. Fingers have energy. Articulation is an act of eloquence.

We have such a misconception. We face the day with a confused mind. Confusion is a condition, an infusion of fragmentation.

The gods and demons are brothers. But only goodness gives life. The Divine dispensation is not a demonical compensation.

Vicious thinking is to say "because I can." Think before you take a step. When you do, be very careful. Look twice before you leap. Thought comes in many ways, with anger, with submissiveness, with the caricatures of lust. The amplification of moral rectitude makes life beautiful and enables us to walk with life even with strange calamities and coercive conditions.

Life has two aspects: simplification or amplification.

All the "gods" are principles and elements contained within you. They are archetypes in the functional family of God. These principles are different energy forces in your body. They give energy to perform this and that. These principles reside in us, but we don't care for them.

Pity leads to insipid dementia. The fundamentals to lead a life of tranquility are foreign. We become natural to devilishness and feeling is completely engrossed in worldly activities. An antiquated mind cannot equate.

Truth itself is positive. Negation is nothing but negating yourself. The fear of oneself is fear of the demonical. There is a demonical fear of the demonical. We try to compromise with the demonical, which increases the fear. Fear comes due to attachment. We must be bold enough to face it, and tell the person who needs to hear it. Often a person who is demonical does not know it. Be yourself and not their selves. We have a bashfulness and axe to grind, and do not tell the truth. In psychological compromise, we go by the tenet of the moment. Truth is open always. Cooperation should listen to what is right.

The negative mind can be deleterious, delirious, or demented. Because we do not know ourselves, we become dependent on someone's thought. Conceit is corruption. Fame is short lived. One day your faults and sins will overtake you. Sins are injurious to health, mind, friendships, and living conditions.

Everyone is a comedian; everyone has committed sin and has shortcomings. Dante never thought something was troublesome. If you have that mentality, then you enjoy life.

The enemies of the Self and their opposites are:

Anger and wrath with the opposite, forgiveness.

Carnal lust (like a sticky salamander) with the opposite, chastity (calm abstinence).

Greed with the opposite, charity (giving not attached to results but for beneficial outcome).

Pride (egotism) with the opposite, humility (simplicity, nobility).

Gluttony with the opposite, temperance (with *pratyahara* or detachment from sensory experience).

Sloth (lazy lumber) with the opposite, zeal (industriousness).

And another is envy with the opposite, compassion.

Chanting mantras gives a noble stature to the brain, and your brain cells will travel beyond you. You go beyond every thought you think, and then all your thoughts will think of you.

In chanting mantras, you cook the brain on the sacrificial fire of life. Mantras channel through the brain, and the sparks occupy the whole system of cells and subatomic particles.

A word is a powerful interaction between existence and non-existence.

When you chant the mantras correctly, there is space inside you. And these mantras can transcend space. Mantra creates a vibration that goes before you. This vibration goes into every sphere, through twelve stages into space. They can even be heard in Russia, where they have an interest in the useful side of yoga.

Sing your chants and mantras, and the mind will not be vicious. All these chants can be recited at any time of the day, in whatever mood you are: It doesn't matter whether you are in an ordinary mood, or a defiant mood, or a refined mood.

Figure 44

I don't know is a great answer!

A lot of people are over corrected.
If one becomes cowed down,
one becomes cowed due to the comments of others.

The knowledge
human beings
accumulated over
so many centuries
created a lot of confusion
because knowledge becomes
a barrier to realize
the essential nature of
a whole being.
You see the dark side,
this wounded child;
everything is a product of that
psychology.
When a person is confused,
a person is confusion itself.
Who is confused? The mind.
Mind is what a person
is in the modern age;
too much mental activity.
We live in the mind, talk in the mind,
speak in the mind.
Who does all those things? It's the mind.
Suppose the mind doesn't mind itself.
What happens?
Instead of minding
itself in all circumstances,
it minds others business.
When you do that you create friction
and a comparison. There is a confusion.
The confused minds says I want to get clarity,
to know that. When that very mind analyses
things, it analyses confusion.
Confusion analyzing confusion.

Figure 45

Facing and Refining the Ego (A Cascade of Quotes)

"I know" is the greatest ego. When you understand the truth behind this, something opens up, an understanding of the inspirational sequence, with no gap, welling up from the origin. When steeped in ignorance, we do not see this and try to defend ourselves.

Resistance is self-aggrandizement. The ego works in a cycle and encircles your heart, your mind. Then you are consumed.

People who never believe in the spiritual have their hearts in a stupor. The mind is masquerading. They talk about false things and ruin their own and other's lives. They suppress the truth and spread falsehood. This is the path of destruction.

This is the age of self-aggrandizement when everyone tries to defend themselves and hide their discontented souls. It is an age of politicians. Empires were built on false premises. Others follow them like dumb driven cattle, not just literally follow but follow to a great fall. This dependence is dangerous. Self-abnegation is self-destruction. The political arena is powerfully in the sway of opinions. The present time is the right time to express the Self and not hide. Be bold enough.

Brutal utter honesty antagonizes the brutally dishonest. Truthfulness needs to have a solid background. This is not just the sharing of opinion. First be grounded. Have a strict, proper, unassailable conviction. Resolve is an inspirational, uncalculated, integrated force that brings reconciliation. You should be convinced in yourself. Honesty should have that force, that fire with reverence for that person. You have to see to whom you are speaking. That is the art form. Honesty tolerates. Telling the truth is a sacrifice. Sacrifice is not abandoning oneself; it is a loving act of giving oneself to God.

Hate hits back. In eternity, all ends meet, and the end is a beginning. There is no end to anything except meeting in eternity.

Before the crumbling, there is a rumbling.

A death wish is a longing for the death of the ego.

The ego is a transferred epithet.

The ego litigates and does not mitigate.

A person becomes conceited and egotistical because of an inferiority complex. The mind has placed itself in a cocoon, a prison. We decorate ourselves inside an attic. We build a palace infested with rats. It is a cocoon cacophony.

We are utterly ordinary because we have no order. How do we bring order in ourselves? We need an emancipatory reflection of our own soul.

The ego is associated with body identity. Experiences come to kill the ego. Good people have tragedies to keep them in line. Everybody wants ambition and tries to establish an identity and loses themselves in indemnity, becoming idiosyncratically imbecilic. There is no guilt greater than to sanction (negative) ambition. This body is not yours. You didn't make it.

Humanity is isolated from the real essence. The ego has created a long path away from this.

You collect all these personalities, which speak not you. When the personalities chatter, it means that you have lost yourself to all these personalities. It is better not to editorialize about our life. A running commentary comes from the modifications of mind. A personality is dejection. A personality is built on what you are not. The externality of the human personality is ambiguity.

A demonical ego has the hunger for power.

The dissolution of the ego depends upon the evolution of the soul and the expansion of consciousness. Evolution is a purgative to bring us to pure thought. "They who humble themselves shall be preserved entire. They who bend shall be made straight. They who are empty shall be filled. They who are worn shall be renewed. They who have much shall go astray." The honorable way is to know "only God is." Meditation with devotion attached to Divine grace pulls the consciousness up in verticality that has no height. Intent on devotion is pertinent intent.

How can you be one with God when you are not one with your Self? That is a falsehood. All is there. One moment can alter your direction. Can you catch that moment? The ego does not allow you to catch that moment. It obstructs. The ego is the scattered mind. It has an idiosyncratic existence. You cannot demolish the ego unless you have gratitude and peace in great proportions that are eternally vast. The ego has fear of the expansive vastness. The original contemplations transcend even contemplation and ascend to a height that cannot be measured. The vertical has no limit.

The limit of ego is the fixated attachment to identity. But the cosmic serpent of time, *Ananta*, wears unlimited cycles of time. We've got pride in our intellect, our understanding, thinking we are great... "I can manage this; I can do this," all the things we say. That's all short lived. You may be a king for five minutes... or five days... or five years, then the kingdom is gone.

We can ultimately reach the truth, and then we realize there is only one truth in a thousand falsehoods. Truth has a premium on it. But we want to have our own way and start bargaining and gain the bar only. Real sacrifice is to surrender the negative tendencies and allow the flowering of goodness.

Seven million years ago the human being was burnt by the eye of *Kakulagislaletomeklometali*, a sage. The ego entered the psyche and cannot be disciplined. It doesn't know what it's doing!

We are peptides in the body of God. You are the connecting link between "That" and "This." So you can be the connecting link between reality and mythology.

We unconsciously encroach upon our freedom and free flow of life. Life is a free flow of beauty. It is a sonorous magnificent lullaby, ever flowing into the ocean of bliss [that] you are. Real reflection is an extraction of life's essence. Your supplication is to your essence, where everything can be decomposed down to its essence. Individuation is an indivisible essence, a continuous flow into the expansive ocean of the Divine. Every person is connected. Your essence is Divine. That quintessence is a supreme order where all is subsumed. The nearest to that supreme order in the human is the inspirational supplicate order. When you supplicate, you super implicate the Divine and regenerate that whole essence into yourself.

Due to soul conditioning in the world, the soul has lost its tremendous capacity. It has to wander. The ego is the fuel of the soul. Ultimately, it is eaten away.

When the ego's center collides the circumference falls off, and the person becomes a real human being. A being of humaneness should involve itself in life. Then it will join the evolving universality of consciousness. Then the person will be one with the universality of consciousness.

On Equating Oneself with a Fragmentary Identity

Even the incarnated gods cannot grasp what is beyond the absolute. We cannot grasp the formless when we are in form. We have that grabbing capacity, but we lose the grip on ourselves! We always want to grab something. We cannot grab Him, That.

The dream was to dream to bring forth something like Himself. I am not using the word "create." There was no form or formlessness. It is a never-ending, dancing, ever fulfilling consciousness, and the power of consciousness. That moved to bring forth "something like Me." He brought forth something to hold all of these, for them to wave, to dance, to sing, to sway. He wanted something to sway, so He created the wind from His own breath. Breath is that ever flowing consciousness. It flows but had nothing to flow over. The air was cool and nice but needed space to hold it. That great energy made dolls and figurines sway. The fanning of eternal, everlasting consciousness became life. That's what we call eternal consciousness, the breath of life. It is also called the web of life. The everlasting consciousness formed all of these.

Something was needed to sustain these. He formed fire, the thermal imprudence! So came heat. Then something to quench this was needed. Water arose. Then something came to sustain it, so the earth was formed. Creation was actually a bringing forth. He looked at all these things and said, "They are not like me, 'not this, not this, not like this person or that person.' I should pervade all these things, and then I will be there! It will be like I am in all these things I brought forth or will bring forth in the future." Then when He looked at each person, He saw his reflection, that is the Soul of God that is the Seal of the Soul.

Shristhi Stiti Laya is the creation, existence in time and space, and the absorption of existence. You have a position. You position yourself as a human being. Then the absorption, *Laya*, is not destruction but absorption, a going to the core.

It is wonderful to associate oneself with the emerging and emanating properties of the core. Geometrically, there is no past, present, or future. Each moment fully lapses and covers the previous one. You are a movement in that eternal moment.

We think existence is a tussle. Why are we born? What is the purpose of life? Where are we going? We ask these questions to everyone, to others, to our professors, our preceptors. We are never satisfied with the answers. We travel and travel and travel for 84 million years. Ultimately, that core catches us.

People say they have a midlife crisis, although no one really knows when that occurs. Life can be 40 years or 80 years. At some point, we get all the memories. They revolve in a circle like figurines and statues. You realize you don't know anything about yourself. You look in the mirror and see your emaciation, your struggles. You have food but worry about what you have the next day. That is avarice.

Your longevity depends upon your longing. You long for wealth, fame, position, stocks etc., but you repent. You say, "I didn't do that good thing when it was possible for me to do it." Human fluctuations lead the human mind to misjudge what to do. Then you have an attitudinal crisis that needs attitudinal healing. It is not a crisis of consciousness, it is an attitudinal crisis. It depends upon what attitude you have, what you cherish to have as a rising star, what you want to have as a staff of life.

Attitude is a gravitational force. If you have the right attitude, you become bold-hearted, *dhrti*, with patience and fortitude. Your mind is strong. Then you can say, "I'm like Him." If your attitude is refined, it reflects the Divine Glory in its resplendent luster. Your face will have that luster. You exude that splendor, what you call your core. This makes you valueless in the world. There is no value to it. We all have that stamp of the invaluable.

We're all leaves on the tree of life. Do you want to be a ghoul or ghost on that tree and be a laughingstock? A great poet Ben Jonson said, "It is not growing like a tree in bulk doth make man better be..." and then Longfellow said, "Life is real! Life is earnest! And the grave is not its goal."

We need an earnest understanding attitude. Last week I spoke about how we seduce ourselves into addiction and reduce ourselves. We sink deeper and deeper into the seduction, going even beyond our capacity to seduce ourselves. Seduction is not just sexual. Depression is one of the products of seducing ourselves. Psychosis begins with the seed of corruption. That seed grows into a tree in the mind. The corrupt seeds grow in the minds of the persons who seduce themselves. There is the destruction. We have to get rid of that. Psychologists have to help to remove the stain, the scar. Patients go through pain, privation, and torture by remembering. Antidepressants just lull the mind into forgetting. It is only a temporary amnesia. First there is the repression, then the suppression, then the depression. Both doctor and patient should leave the false stand. The patient should leave the disease and the doctor should lead. Before the disease was the human being. Can you go to the origin without identifying with the disease?

We need to go in the right direction. We have been put forth and not created. You have to solve the mystery. I have given all the clues. These are the conditions you have, and you live them. In living those conditions, you are not at ease. We become obsessed with possibilities, even those that are not possible for us. Our whole energy is invested in the obsessions, and society supports them in the name of progress. Persons make money but destroy the whole life. At least some people realize this. It is hard to convince someone who is ignorant. The answer is in the obsession. It depends upon your development. For development you have to work hard or just try to understand. Sometimes it is not feasible to understand. The conscious equation makes it not feasible. You equate yourself with something and deny the reality. Instead of "not this," we say "It (or I am) is this." We try to satisfy ourselves through a defense. The thought of the world is not the world itself. We convict ourselves through a conviction and become convicts and con-victims!

Life is a play, but a very serious play, and we are like children. There is a door in the wall of the garden. If one has courage, Godly independence, when passing now and then peep through the door and imagine what might be in it – and walk through that door! To understand duality is Absolute Reality. That is non-duality. Then you can play with it, cooperate with it, and love it. That is where love starts. You go beyond your limitations and know your place.

Satsang Talk on September 9, 2001
(Final line from talk August, 1994)

One must be very careful to establish oneself in goodness. It may not prevent oneself from doing wrong, but it will enable the realization to correct oneself quickly. Your sins follow you, and your good deeds precede you.

Any sound that falls upon us, from the sky, or any corner of creation, even trees and birds, whispers and tells us something. Everything has got a sound, even a deaf person has sound, even though he cannot hear it.

Figure 46

On Sanity (A Cascade of Quotes)

Spirituality is utter, downright sanity.

Rescue your Self at every step from Self-negation.

Sanity is the tip of the intelligence.

Be a clear thinker, a hard worker, a generous and compassionate human being. Help others if you can. Have a generous heart and a tranquil mind and think good thoughts always. God is a good thought. Think about whoever your God is.

Anger is insanity. If you want to retaliate, observe silence, persevere in patience. Refinement is the most wonderful thing!

Mindfulness is to be full of the Divine, so nothing else creeps in. The Divine cannot be divided. It is not divisible. There is nothing provisional, nothing optional; therefore, it is called Absolute.

If you make your Self possible, then it's possible not to think.

We neglect the simple things and want to go into the complex. We need to be sane always.

Over extending oneself is abandoning the Self.

The mind is an indomitable aspect of life. You must be in touch with your brain. When fear comes, you are not in touch with your brain.

The brain is an intern of the heart. It acts on what you put into it. It doesn't have a mind of its own.

You have to think about the whole world. The whole world is unreal, under the sway of unreal conditions and not knowing any other way. But we are the authors of our conditions.

How do you build a life in a hostile world? In spite of everything changing every day, the elements themselves don't change. Human cruelty and intolerance have the advantage of suppressing the weak and becoming predominately powerful. Then the powerful produce indulgence and nefarious acts.

When the faithless become cruel, faith will ordain you to become faithful to your Self.

You must first be grounded in a strict, proper, and unassailable conviction. The essential nature of goodness causes a vibration of energy. Goodness is a Divine potency, but one cannot be totally good in the world. The ego has to balance itself with goodness.

Collect all the scattered currents of your life and direct them toward your dear Self, which is God.

Scriptures, like the four *Vedas*, are heard from the universal sound. Sages considered them *Bhagavatam*, the Lord. Scripture can only be inwardly understood. If you concentrate on a scripture, you will know the meaning. In yoga, you develop so much concentration that whatever you want to know, you will know. You become the vehicle of understanding.

The *Puranas* are epic stories not scriptures. Poetic license pushes the poet's own ideas in a romantic way.

The world is intellectual. The intelligent do not fall into the power struggle. Intellectuality is jealous because of comparison. It tries to compete with God's mandate and caring process for the world. When the intellect tries to go beyond its limit, it is debarred and has to surrender. When the mind goes beyond the intellect, it falls into a different category, the creative and inspirational. Then it is out of the ordinary.

Intelligence pierces everything, including the confusion of fame and intoxication. Politicians are separatists. Separation is the problem in the world. We in our innocence and skepticism succumb to it. One should not have conceit or self-centeredness. Happiness is a birthright. Unhappiness is acquired. To be happy in all this conflict is to be humble, sincere, without duplicity and dehumanization. Then the growth flows from the human mind to the universal mind to the Divine.

Free yourself from yourself. Permit your Self to wage war against your anti-Self. Stay evil and promote good. Renounce much. Accept little. "A man who knows he is a fool is not a great fool. A man who knows his error is not greatly in error."

We should not allow our thoughts to migrate. When they do migrate, we get a migraine!

If we follow the dictates of our own pure consciousness, we are equated with the truth. You render yourself impure through the contamination of ideas. Pure consciousness is the pure unpolluted thought process that leads through the real understanding of creation and onto real emancipation.

Sense and sensibility must go together. When we are not sensible, then we make the senses sensational and de-centralize ourselves. There are so many attractions in the world, the senses are torn apart and carried away. When you attract something, you repel something.

Smell indicates purity. *Vishnu's* heaven has a heavenly scent. A bad smell indicates decay. If heaven has not begun for us it is because we established a false consciousness by imagining heaven is something that begins after this life. It is our own dualistic way of envisioning our life. There is a heaven in every human heart in the fullness of spring. Real heaven has an original smell, your original scent. Saints and sages have a beautiful scent, a shaped and scented perfume by the original hand of God that is not artificial.

The only things that will help you are those words that come out of the heart and soul of the Holy Ones who express themselves with the mandate of the one God. Their every cell reverberates with consciousness.

Without Grace, diseases increase. Disease is the warning of the mental aberration.

Saints may suffer but don't complain because they have the strength of the Divine.

Ascended masters made their body suitable for the Divine presence.

A relentless mind is a reckless mind. A goal-less mind is a guile-less mind.

With individuality comes the science of life. You are your own measure. Our individuality is so far from us, we are divided scarecrows. We compare and compute, falling into jealousy and foolishness.

Everybody has at least two personalities, negative and positive. Self-abnegation is to diminish the linkage you have to the Divine process, limitless exuberance, and compassion. You can overcome the negative by the positive, once you ascertain these. Then you surrender to the noble personality that is good, charitable, equitable, and most pleasing. All pathways meet in compassion. It is a reliable radiance with great passion or rather with an impassioned, all-pervading essence of ecstasy.

The culprit in passion is the separation.

The worth of life is passion from compassion, the essential nature of God. Christ had this. It is the passion for goodness. Holy water sprang from the eyes of Jesus Christ. His religion is the symbolic goodness of a man who asked for that great kindness and compassion and rose to the height of his Father. He covered the whole horizon on Easter. He covered the whole horizon of life.

We are in vastness, but we have a fear of that expansion. The undivided truth is that awareness continues to exist.

The most you can expect from your friends is nobility of purpose. Implement your nobility to inspire humility. Then you don't expect anything else.

Don't be a hypocrite. Be first what you say with that nobility of purpose.

Take it for granted that you are granted.

Spirit is all inclusive. When we come to all confusion, we cannot conclude. When life is grounded by external knowledge it always results in confusing attitude and atmosphere. How much confidence is in you? What tendency do you bring out in yourself? What is the impact of the externals? We cultivate those externals. In every movement you produce something. You cannot be without production, or you go into reduction. When you are established in your Self, in nature, in the order of law, of God, it always saves you from all calamities. Your mind is not the mind, it must be de-minded.

A still mind is still active. There is a play of the still mind.

Without proper food, the mind falls into a vibratory confusion. Mind matters! If not composed of the right matter, it multiplies and becomes wavering, puzzled, and confused.

To be happy always is the panacea of all ills. Care for your suffering brethren. But a caring person can also be easily carried away.

With attraction and repulsion, enjoy the dazzle but do not succumb to it.

Overturn what is happening in the world and make a good turn.

You are the archer. You are the target.

Authorities do not help. We succumb to them. Where is the pure Self?

It's a good thing not to think. Thinking causes turmoil inside. Be infrared rather than drawing inferences.

How do you know who you are? Every name has a vibration. Why identify with a particular name? We become so patterned. We want to become something because we don't know how to be. How do you know you deserve a particular name? In reality, God said you are nameless. We name God also and have fragmented that, adhering to falsehood. Then we try to talk through the falsehood. We try to manipulate the result and try to change it and start another falsehood. Christians do not believe in Christ. Buddhists do not even pronounce his name correctly. A name should correspond to the behavior. We try to achieve a name to get respect from the public but don't deserve the name.

Go inside, in your heart of hearts, not with an eccentric idea but a concentric idea.

Life has become untruth. Ignorance involves different types of temporary identification. When enmeshed in ignorance, then you don't listen to anyone. It kills the neurons. The neurons should get inspiration from your knowledge. The heart is the seat of God. The mind wanders. If you succumb to that wandering, you lose the power of intelligence. From untruth, go to truth. Lose your arrogance, egotistic attitudes, and ignorance. From there you become a world citizen.

Examine your life. When truthfulness is applied to the Self, you expose your own secret with your last answer. After you have exhausted yourself with all the answers, then you're your Self. That is meditation. Look for the minute corruption link in the chain of light. Do not compromise with your examination. Do not say, "Tomorrow I will change." That change never comes.

From experience you get some knowledge of your mistakes! You go on repeating a behavior and get disgusted and tired of it. You go on eating the same food and become disgusted. If you study your own history, you gain discriminative power when it has a rich background of sincerity. This needs serenity, sincerity, and the absence of vanity. We become so cheap before the personality. Sincerity is a science, and insincerity is a non-science. Then we try to manipulate and don't have smooth sailing. We then ask why and form another concept [that] is false because it is built upon false premises. When you are a bit vain, you try to hide something. This is not about your appearance but about lying to impress others. With real impressiveness, you are truthful, which creates an atmosphere of awe. When you try to hide from yourself, you become awful.

To take advantage of a failure and short fall is to be centralized. Mathematically the two contradictions become one. Then the center is gone, the mind is then only expansion.

The yogis understood that the confrontation with the self is to be truthful. Every morning they conducted an exercise in self-inquiry. To admit mistakes unequivocally is to make no excuses. Mistakes come from not paying attention, but rather being full of tension, defying awareness. If people do not confess first to themselves, their actions represent a confession that coincides with depression.

And if they try to repress the depression, it becomes oppression. To reflect ignorance is to deflect awareness. When awareness is deflected, people do not admit ignorance and become accustomed to being symptomatic.

There is no meaning in a false apology. Do not bring shame on yourself. Contrition is a real confession. Simplicity, sincerity, absence of vanity, and purity bring health and happiness.

If you reflect on yourself, take note of all you've done and think. To be able to be honest, you may need "open heart surgery." If you try to cheat yourself, you don't remember. Then comes dementia.

The combined effort of goodness creates a vortex of immunity, utility, and emancipation. There is a continuous flow of goodness in eternity and consciousness when there is honesty and truth, without a lot of reproaches.

Do not use your mind power to condemn or praise yourself. Then the mind becomes sublime. You don't own your sin. You become a fresh person and gain insight. You become sacrosanct. Then only are you able to advise others.

In real self-study, you ask yourself to be absolved from all sins and all your stress. These are not to dwell upon. Blame, shame, and regret can be sentimental perversions. Perversion is a decomposed compulsion. God is the only one who will never commit a sin. Simply surrender it all to God. Confess and say, "Please pardon me." To examine oneself squarely and fairly, and to offer these up, is the surrender. Be familiar with your God. He'll take it.

How do you maintain that goodness? What is good to nature is good. There needs to be a cooperative movement for this with nothing pilfered.

I Surrender My Speech, My Mind, My Sensory Impressions - My Higher Mind-Even My Nature to the Supreme One (on CD Satyam Shivam Sundaram)

Kaayena Wachaa Manasendri Yairwaa, Budhyatamanaava Prakriti Swabhavaatth

Whatever I do physically, whatever I do with work and through all senses

Karomi Yad Yad SaKakalam Parasmai, Naarayanaa Yeti Samrpayaam I

Through natural instincts I offer all to you, great One, my defects, my all –
You take care of it

Anything I do with body and mind, I offer all to you my Lord

(One always does good things when offering to God – holiest of holies)

Even artists and other professions have cooperative ventures, but there is a lot of jealousy and hatred because someone becomes powerful. This leads to a lot of diseases.

A multiple approach helps sanity. It is not mine or yours, but the consciousness itself does a great work to immunize the system of love. This has been trodden upon, lead astray, hurt, and injured.

A single approach is selfishness embroidered with so called great works. Selfishness causes molecular dispersion. We go on doing what is not applicable. Consciousness has a different approach. When we do wrong, there is a reproach. When we go wrong, it changes the vibration of the cells. This is pollution. We feel we should have known.

Think about your personal life. How much falsehood do you support? Dishonesty breeds dishonesty. Ill breeds ill. How much truth do you neglect? In your family obligations do you condone untruth? There is a method of conniving untruth. Young people should consider mending their life. If everyone would do it, the world would be truthful and established in the Self. Learn good habits and better mind training. Then you find the goodness of your heart, the enormity of your mind, resistance to the temptations, and you are able to live an exemplary life.

Strengthen yourself in your faith and in expressing your truth. For this you must be strong, earnest, and honest. There is nothing to confess. You are a replica of the Godhead, a replica on earth. No one is perfect, not even God. There is a hope that we will all transcend and become transcendental beings. Transcendence is not complete until you transcend even the idea of the gods. Don't lose it. There may be difficulties, but you are a temple of the tenant who resides in your body. His rent is goodness. Do not defraud Him. Pay the rent with faith, dexterity. Do not proceed like dumb, driven cattle. *Sadhasaviveka* is discernment. It is a great mind set. It is free and gathers all knowledge of perfection. Slavery can be savory. Love your truth, and emancipate your treachery and slavishness. The only way to go beyond good and evil is through the good. "Do good" to all of creation. Give more than you take. It is good to do charity to a worthy person. There are rules of right behavior and respect. You can be polite but not political. There is a sense of discipline. Sometimes a person can be gruff out of love, pushing someone away to bring them back.

The gist of life is right knowledge. The zest of life is right action. We have a lot of fear, fear of being in a difficult position. The gut feeling is important. The heart feeling can be loose and go here and there. The heart is subject to failure. Do not condemn your body with the turmoil of hatred, jealousy, and negative emotions. Keep it soft and pliable. This basic principle of resistance and not yielding has resilience and a *raison d'etre*. Then the heart becomes permeable but not vulnerable or succumbing to temptation. Guts have "guts." Then we are not afraid. There is a firm, standardized spiritual and impactful instinct hidden inside human life. The psyche is ever expanding and extensive. The gist is the sum total; like a seed it expands. The puzzling things in the human race seem unsolvable with deep divisions, foolishness, and fragmentation. But the guts cannot be fragmented. Right knowledge infuses an understanding of resourcefulness. It gives a happy feeling, a laudable attitude to do the right thing. If you have zest to do the right thing, there is the understanding that every point of life is in the light.

A logical understanding of the self is not to have logic! Logic can be illogical if preached by an illogical person. We seek a logical explanation of illogical life. We do not lead an inspirational life.

Weigh and see how good your *gurus* (teachers) are. Weigh them and come to an understanding, not a conclusion. Learn to use proper words and then keep quiet! The word *Sarasvati* (the goddess of knowledge) [is] to be respected.

Assess another person by how truthful they are, how much strength they have.

People go to *sadhus* (holy men) and fall at their feet, but discriminate what you receive. You can be friendly with them but be careful. Many are wolves in sheep's clothing.

The future is not to be wanted. The part is not to be sought. Extend health, and do not seek a reward.

A composed life is well composed, firm, and dear to God. Not condoning oneself means to repent when truth dawns. Energy applied correctly is spiritual energy, surrendered to God, and will do the right thing.

Truth is the ambassador of life.

Penance is a fitting, amply correct sacrifice, a burning of all mistakes by austerities. True penance is total selflessness. Real repentance burns up all the wrongdoing.

Unfortunately, many demons move the god through intense penance. The god (*Shiva*) is moved and bestows boons. But the boons and powers corrupt. Yoga is a universal science and forms a universal community. Real yogis do not crave power.

All have that sacrificial instinct until selfishness arises after great grief and privation. But even animals surrender when they are helpless.

Always think beyond your thought. There is always darkness under the candle.

If someone says, "I don't want to know all those things," I say that is fine with me. Just refine yourself, redefine yourself; rebuild yourself and your life. Put fresh building blocks, and make sure you have a heliport at every step to jump off!

Not to dupe yourself is most important. Do not stand on pretense but on your ground of love, sincerity, and amicability. To grope in darkness is only to grab the darkness.

Start from the beginning. Yoke yourself to God, not to human beings. Be honest with yourself and start anew. Make your purpose righteous and dignified. Life is a good will mission. Your mission is what you create from your gifts. The real mission does not take but gives. Stars are the flowers of the Tree of Life. Your life should be like a starlit sky and the glory of morning.

Without cherishing life, there is no pursuit of Yoga or the union of body, mind, and Spirit. Without their peaceful union, there is no accumulation of merit. Without merit or worthiness, the Spirit does not bestow pure insight. Without cherishing life and merit, life itself is not lived but is consigned to mediocrity and ineptitude.

The majesty of life is the tapestry of living, inspired by the One to whom the heart belongs, who is always in my heart.

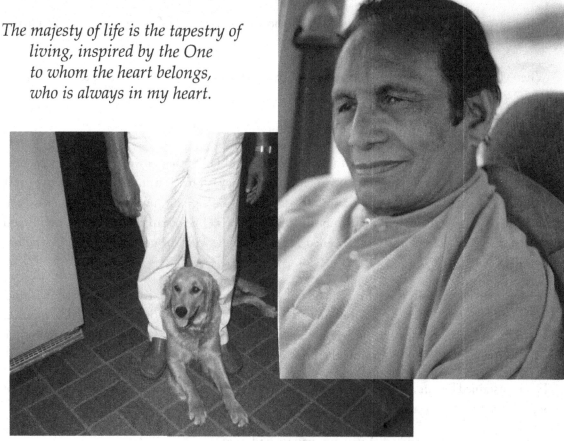

Figure 47

Toward Realization (A Cascade of Quotes)

Rhapsody Reverberating Everywhere: That is Your Destination

One is all that is, was, and will be. The cipher is zero. Zero down on yourself.

The Divine ego is selfless. It lifts you up. It has no seed (*Sabhij*) to require you to come back to earth. If you are absorbed (*Laya*) in that it is *Nirbij*, without seed.

Awareness is energy.

Give up your ego patterns of thinking that you are wise and have talents. All these things lead to misery.

One real deep prayer is enough to make the arrogance, false ideas, and ego fall away, like a snake shedding its skin.

Abide in truth and goodness, and the Lord will abide in you.

It is not to know or understand that is important, but realizing. Taking refuge in the Self is total surrender; then comes realization.

Nothing works. The No-Thing works. With no props, you are left with the core. You'll not change, unless you are on the edge.

When you are aware, that is what you are. Truth is not what you think you are, but what you are made of. Nobility in life begins with oneself. It is a succession from pettiness.

Life is lofty if you are not crafty. After the nobility, comes mobility.

Do not think you have to compromise to get honor and fame; that is weakness. Glory in your being indispensable. Do not pine for that which you don't have. That is unnecessary. You have great riches in you. Never lose your courage and human dignity. Be vigilant, not fearful. Otherwise you will be sucked away by the current, which brings all the debris. The ocean throws out all debris and only keeps the gold. That is why God is called *Hirianyagarbha* with the golden womb, He who has a belly full of gold.

Believe in your own ability. Realize you are not what you appear to be. Know how to laugh, smile, and be simple, tolerant, and grateful for your origin, which is no-thing but has substance, essence, and life. The strength and drive behind your ability is the essence of God. That reverberation of the human substance produces and sustains the universe.

Life is sustained by our ability to take care of ourselves with reverence, respect, honesty, and right action. That is the way to sustain life, to take care of oneself adequately and not excessively.

When you know who and what you are, you won't know.

My radiance will hold me in the rainbow of God.

The earth is the celestial cow that gives everything. It is the only planet where you can learn everything because it tolerates everything. You can learn all the *yogas* here as well as compassion, kindness, cruelty. This learning is the principle of *Karma Yoga*. Even the gods came to earth to enjoy this. The earth is called *Karma Bhumi*, the land of action.

Why did Nero celebrate while Rome burned? He was glad the sin was being removed. Fire is the greatest purifier. Nothing can sit on top of fire. Not [even] a fly who can sit on everything. Truth is like a great fire. Nothing burns like fire. Nothing inspires like the truth.

Scientists find that the stratosphere has a vibration that inspires always.

An astounded mind is a calm mind. An astounded mind has no place for deprivation.

To be in tune with your spirit, you have to see your worth and the strength behind it, which is balance, which is God. Then your faith will not hang in the balance. Balance only comes from serious meditation where the meditator is absent. Then there is only energy, grace, joy, and emancipation. Your birthright is to have these. Your elegance is to enjoy them. Your propensity is to spread them. Your delightful attitude is to guide it with a sublime, noble, delectable mind. Don't try to delete the grace. Don't welcome something not suitable to you. Elect all these qualities to tackle your sorrow.

The intellectual mind is arrogant, isolated from the mainstream. Individuality is undivided.

The intelligent mind is sublime.

The point of friction is the point of union.

Without injury there is no happiness. Truth as the ultimate reality will bring liberation and freedom. It takes indomitable courage to speak the truth. You may think it will hurt someone, but if it hurts it may liberate that person.

When you stand in the character of your Divine endowment, you do not have major problems.

Sufficiency and contentment bring an enduring and unchanging simplicity. Sincerity and morality are scientific.

The *Tao* is the unknowable, unthinkable, and untouchable. Simplicity brings the absence of desire. The absence of desire brings serenity and tranquility of mind. A tranquil heart and mind brings peace and no perversion. This is how to make the mind restful. With the name of God comes the right chemical in the brain.

God does not want anything from you. Is God indifferent? No. He is everywhere. If we separate ourselves from consciousness, we do not get anything. God is not an entity. He is all pervading Spirit.

God is sexless. There is no sex problem, only a fixed problem, to keep you on the right path and to join you on that path, leading you to your ultimate goal, emancipation.

The universal Supreme, the Lord Magnificent Divine remains in your heart, permeates the cells of the body like *Hanuman* who said to *Rama*, the Lord, "My hair stands on end, every hair of my body is in you, and sings Your Name."

Buddhists speak about *Nirvana* and they mean the void, [while] Hindus prefer *Mukti*, or Liberation. There you completely dissolve in what you call God. When you dissolve, you will not be able to say, "I have dissolved!" So when one dies you will not get up and say, "I am dead."

To reach God, you must have utter sensitivity and be one pointed. It must have a vertical movement. This is a sensitivity that is not limited by the external. This pierces the veil of *Maya* (Illusion) and goes beyond it to the truth. Try to see beyond what you think. See the inner meaning in the everlasting.

Real perception is at the core of being. What we are made of is at the real core, which is not porous.

You have got to get inside knowledge… I don't know how they arrive at that, "unconscious," and "subconscious," "consciousness," and "unconsciousness." Jung ultimately, when he became very old, actually retracted his steps and said a funny thing. Who said unconscious? It is awareness. If you think there is unconsciousness, the consciousness always dreams of the unconscious, and the unconscious also dreams of the consciousness… and who witnesses this is Awareness. The observer has no perception… the observer is the observed. That's again God. The observer is the observed. You are that Awareness; you must know that. You are beyond consciousness and unconsciousness both, therefore you are the observer: Observe that you are aware, you are aware. Then what happens, you bridge the gulf between what you think is conscious and unconscious and makes it aware. So there's nothing but awareness.

Real emancipation comes at the right moment, with the right thing, at the right juncture, and with the right calculation. Being real and truthful brings emancipation. There is a precise order. It has an utter sensitivity that brings inspirational outbursts to cover all of your shortcomings. The right thing coming at the right time is in the context of Divine dispensation. Then you are above what you are now.

You are the round and ground. You are bound by the ground. When you are bound, you only experience in the silence of consciousness. Accumulation manifests as God according to one's capacity. God is so vast. There is no way to catch That.

Like Ramakrishna, you can become a disciple to experience the essence. We try to obtain the inspirational emancipation. We try to emancipate ourselves to the greatest freedom, but we are not inspired. If you really put one foot into it, you'll be swept away. The question comes, where do you put the foot?! In the *Upanishads*, they saw everything is "not This." At one point you stop, and this becomes That, and That is what you need!

When you undertake a journey, you start at your home. A real home is where your stamina for spirituality lies. Any home should be "where nothing touches me." We are here to solve the puzzle. There is no definition for kindness. Now you go to the beginning. What is that beginning of me and you? To be knowledgeable means that we have spread out our life in an existential way. All the ingredients make you whole.

We come to existential preparedness. First you must be convinced that you exist. Do you know you exist? That is not a thing to be known. Existential bliss is life in an ocean of joy. Sorrow does not enter into the mind. There is no obstruction. *Amrit Tatwa* is the nectar of life, that which cannot die. This is called *Moksha* (liberation). Existential preparedness is that you exist to prepare for non-existence. You find this most clearly in your pets.

A sublime ego is always grateful, like animals. Dogs are from Jupiter, and cats are from the moon. Dogs know that creation is a constant struggle, even to the Creator. They know how to establish rapport between themselves and their owner.

Revolving evolution goes on revolving until it produces the essence, the essentiality of life.

God created humans as Divine compensation. With the force and power of creation, we are created with the ingredients of peace, honesty, equanimity, and prosperity. When all other things enter us, we become demonic. The absence of Divine power is the demon. Artificial power comes from deep ignorance. Overall if you observe yourself, you will see what is missing. When gratitude is not there, no peace is there. Demonical qualities explode into diseases. Even in the face of trouble, be positive and grateful to creation. Nobody has more gratitude than dogs. Dogs link us with the Divine with these qualities: gratitude, purity of heart and mind. The human race came to multiply cooperation, love, and happiness. The multiplicity creates a lot of support. God is a realized experience.

Realization is awareness of the totality of your Self connected to all of life.

When we die, we enter the ocean of bliss. It is a permanent thing going on all the time. Our impediment is thinking. Do not think when we don't think, we are dead. It is not that. When we do not identify with our thoughts, we just let it flow. To recognize the bliss and be one with it is the height of spirituality. Your greatest treasure never depletes. It has sustainability with a one- pointed attitude.

Dr. Shyam
embodied deep
contemplation and dignity.

Figure 48

148

Chapter X

SUMMUN BONUM: THE HIGHEST GOOD

To Speak and To Listen

To speak or not to speak is the question that bothers the speaker. To listen or not to listen is the question that troubles the listener. When doubting questions in the speaker and the listener arise, there is no speaking in depth and no listening in depth. When in both, the doubting questions are removed, [and] there is only speaking and listening. All these movements of speaking and listening are in the living present; therefore, there is only openness, giving, and receptivity. Doubts arise when the mind of the speaker and that of the listeners are in the constant habit of hankering after the scholarly or illusory pursuits of life, hovering around the egoistic propensities of the false, conditioned, and cultivated self. If the speaker has insight into the ground of matter, which is beyond the usual thought process and within the unfathomable depth of infinity, which has order and originality, he can perhaps awaken a similar insight in the mind of the listener. In this there is a profound sharing, great passion, intensity, depth, level, and rationality.

Now the common knowledge, what we call the common knowledge, we cherish in the world is that we are highly civilized, that we need a kind of high speed in all our movements and activities so that we might be able to grab the maximum portion of the world and enjoy life in all its complexities. We need excitement. We need sense titillation at every step we take and at every turn we make. We need to socialize to become popular and in this process of socializing, we de-socialize ourselves and become puppets of desire, crude passions, and irrational idiosyncrasies. We sacrifice our dignity, our morals, our virtues, and our rules to acquire the opposite traits and revel in them till our energies deplete, till we become exhausted. What do you get from all these things? Is it to your advantage?

When our nervous system is wrecked, the natural order of our brain cells is disturbed. We don't find happiness. We suffer. We develop anxiety, we go into depression. Diseases develop. We suffer and suffer. Then what do we do? We seemingly yearn to turn over a new leaf and to have a different movement, a different direction, and a different turn. We then doubtfully say we are on the spiritual path. We are not sure. I'm afraid to use the word spiritual. It is so loaded. But I may point out that this so called new movement starts from the same center, the confused unnatural center of the false self. The negative mind is blind to the center. The *Isha Upansihad* 9th stanza proclaims:

andham tamah praviśanti ye'vidyāmupāsate
tato bhūya iva te tamo ya u vidyāyām ratāh

The meaning is, "Those who worship the illusory pursuits and rites of the world remain enmeshed in the blinding darkness of ignorance. But into denser darkness enter those who are engrossed in the intellectual or psychological pursuits of knowledge for its own sake."

You all know this, this game of life, this game of thinking. Let us be modest in all our endeavors. I have talked in many meditation sessions about the two movements on the path of evolution in relation to human beings: the movement of outgoing or the movement of incoming or returning. These in Sanskrit are the *Pravritti Marga,* or involutionary path, and the *Nivritti Marga,* or the evolutionary path. The involution into matter leads to illusion and ignorance. The deeper you get involved in matter; the deeper is the illusion and ignorance. The evolution to spirit leads to the essential and true nature, which is inherent in us. Good luck and Godspeed.

Talk before a trip to Brazil, 1985

Oh Mighty One

Oh Great One, one day very soon,
the rain will come,
the river will rise,
and I will swim across
to meet You, to greet You,
oh Great One.

Every time I send
my thoughts of gratitude,
they are blown away
by the wind of time.
Like flower petals,
they wither and fall away
before they reach You,
oh Beautiful One.

Some day my soul will ride
the ripples of joy
and the waves of bliss.
My spirit will soar
to the heights of peace
and the depths of love.
And in faith I bow,
oh Glorious One.

My heart will open
and open in earnest
to contain the fury of creation
and the joy of elation,
true to every revelation,
without separation,
oh Mighty One.

Figure 49

Blessing on the Millennium
2000 AD

May the dawn of the new Millennium bring
Peace and prosperity to the created world.

May the unconscionable acts of violence and exploitation cease.

May goodness and harmony prevail and unite
The human race as one global community.

May we all celebrate the glory and splendor of life
In each and every moment of existence and
Join the stars and the planets in spreading light and love.

May we raise Waves of Wisdom and Oceans of Joy
In the Holiness of our Hearts
And the Godliness of our minds and
Extend ourselves gracefully even beyond the Millennium.

Love and Peace,

Shyam

I Love You All
1984

I love you all.
I love you all.
Lights of the New Age,
Stars of heritage,
I love you all.
I love you all.
Flowers of the golden dawn,
Fragrance of the desert lawn,
I love you all.
I love you all.
I love you all.
Not because I say so,
But I love you so.
Life after life,
Year after year,
Day and night,
Even in the candle light,
You have walked the path
Knowing not you have made it all.
Leaning on the shadows of the past,
Lured by the meadows of the vast,
You have walked the path
Knowing not you have made it all.
Not by chance,
Not by luck,
You have made this day yours forever.
You have donned the splendor
Your infinite wonder,
Knowing not you have made it all.
I love you all.
I love you all.
Not because I say so
But because I love you so.

Om Shanti Shanti Shanti Om

Figure 50

A Summation

Editor's Note

As I noted in the Introduction, I do not feel adequate to summarize or paraphrase the essence of the teachings of this remarkable human being and master. Thus, I leave you with his own words about the essence of the human being and human life. Always a humanist as well as a cosmic teacher, Dr. Shyam stressed that the culmination of a refined human life is to be "a fully born human being." With this in mind, we leave you with Shyam's own words.

The Core

Being is knowing, and love is nothing but knowing. The being, which is love, is nothing but knowing. I am coming to that gulf. These are all one. They are all different aspects of the one central core. We say we have to go to that core, to that being. The center of the core is peace. The core is very mischievous; it has got a lot of turmoil, chaos. From what you call chaos the world has come. Yet peace lies in its center. A human being is a miniature universe, a microcosm. All the things you find in the universe, you find in the human being also. The microcosm is engulfed by the macrocosm. It is vast, immeasurable, and immutable, yet ever changing, ever changing except in the center. The center doesn't change. Therefore, it is peaceful. Every other thing around it changes. The center moves, rotates, and whirls but doesn't change. In this great journey as human beings, our own microcosms are engulfed in the macrocosm.

There are always extremes, but the center must be equidistant from the extremes. Even though now estimates are that the earth is about five billion years old, it is some seconds compared to the cosmos. There is a center in the cosmos. If you know yourself, you know where the center is. You know all those things in one tiny step of knowing the center. What is the meaning of taking a step? That step is invisible. It is abstract. In walking you go step by step, putting one foot in front of the other. But here, you do not walk. You stand still. That is the stillness of the mind. It took some time for me to understand. I can have a thought, but do I understand my own thought? This is like taking a step on a step. We make the thoughts, they are separate. Each has a referent, like a morning thought, an evening thought. They come like a garland on a string. That is the process of our life. The main thing human beings do in given circumstances it to accept or reject. These are very natural to life. Acceptance and rejection are two static points. When you go toward rejection, you go from the point of acceptance and vice versa. We don't try to take a middle course. And if you do try to take a middle course, you try to reason. You reason with your thought and then are engulfed in another thought. What happens then is that you are further engulfed in thought. Then you are the thought because you are encircled, bound up in thought. Your whole personality is nothing but thought. You are guided by thought, insinuated by it, enclosed by it. You are standing in the middle as thought. Then what do you do? Therefore, you take a pause. You stand still; you take a step on a step.

We are not surrendered yet. We don't know how, and we doubt whether we will. But you pause. When you reach the step on the step, where you cannot go to one point of acceptance or another point of rejection, you cannot go anywhere. You may try to think again, abstractly, or in a mystified way, or irreverently. But then you become irrational. When you cannot move, you become standstill.

You have come to a point of stillness. You are at the standstill. The mind becomes silent because you have nothing to do. Now where is the center? The mystics say, "Center everywhere, circumference nowhere." The thoughts just stop. Now there is no acceptance or rejection. The only thought may be yourself.

Addiction isolates everything. Addiction appropriates something you have and makes wrong use of it. You are addicted to certain things because there is emptiness, but in absorption you are not isolated. There you assimilate all things. In absorption, there is "wholefulness." You are able to absorb nutrients that are necessary to provide an awakening, an understanding, and clarity in the absorption. When a plant takes in nutrients, it doesn't take all the dirt. It siphons off only what it needs. If you observe the plant, you see that it takes in only clear liquid. If you think you are wanting, you are completely outside yourself. With addiction you want to fill the emptiness inside with something that produces intoxication, a stupor. It can happen in many ways with many things. You become dull and numb. Addiction comes from deprivation and absorption from fullness. Addiction makes a person a slave. You must know how to discriminate between addiction and absorption. Emancipate yourself from your treachery and slavishness.

When you are in the stillness, in the center, the absorption connects to the ocean of nectar, which will never intoxicate but rather helps you to grow and have a good life. You are full because you are getting the nourishment from everything, because you know the art of drawing that nourishment from heaven and earth and from life. There you stand still, an eternal moment in time and space without separation. Like a top, the center, the core, has that tremendous velocity, dynamism, and creative energy. It is the power behind all things. Like the top spinning, it is the top of everything, the first vibration. That is how the universe got started and continues. There is no way you have anything to do, you are not distracted. If you fall out of that stillness, you have to give it a jolt. You must know how to listen to that sound. You are listening to yourself. You must know how to hold onto it. You are complete, you are nothing but love. With addiction, a person is a slave, soulless. In absorption, you are soulful. It makes a person a master. Love frees. Attachment will not free. Love always stands against bondage. That is the love of God. It is humble and very powerful. Absorption is union, and everything else is separation. Absorption is ambrosia, fullness, where you are full of nothing but love.

Satsang talk, 1994

Obituary

SHRIKRISHNA KASHYAP (Dr. SHYAM)

The majestic and magnanimous lion of God, Dr. Shyam, has passed peacefully in his home at 2:34 AM on Saturday, January 31, 2015. His long life of unselfish service to humanity began in the ancient Indian tradition of the science of life, Ayurveda, and led to his practice of severe yogic austerities in a Himalayan cave. With a profound connection to St. Francis of Assisi, he moved to Santa Fe de Santo Francisco de Assisi, New Mexico in 1980, eventually becoming a citizen of the United States. Thousands of devotees throughout the world saw him as a spiritual lightning rod of truth, self-awakening, and integrity. His healing work touched tens of thousands of grateful patients.

His spiritual and healing messages are enshrined in his nonprofit Wisdom Wave, (wisdomwave. org) which will continue to consolidate his teachings in audio, video, and published forms.

One of his memorable messages was simply, "Be good. Do good."

Om Shanti Shanti Shanti Om

Glossary (primarily with Dr. Shyam's definitions)

Achara: Right behavior; part of Dr. Shyam's trinity of right conduct.

Adi Shakti: The primordial power, the feminine energy, the power of pure consciousness.

Agni: The god or principle of fire.

Ahara: Proper food, considered the essence of the human being; part of Dr. Shyam's trinity of right conduct.

Alef or *Aleph:* In the Jewish tradition, the first letter.

Aleef: In Arabic the same thing, *Aleef.*

Amrita Bindu: The nectar point is the indestructible drop beyond the *Atman.* The point comes, then the circle, then the point inside the triangle, which is the first stable form.

Amrit Tatwa: This is the nectar of life, that which cannot die. This is called *Moksha, Mukti* or Liberation. There you completely dissolve in what you call God.

Ananda: Universal Bliss; third part of the Trinity of *Sat* (truth, existence), *Chit* (Consciousness), and *Ananda* (Bliss, love).

Ananda Aditya: The maximum bliss accumulated

Ananta: The cosmic serpent of time, who wears unlimited cycles of time.

Atishiwa: That which comes from the voice of the sky

Atman: Atom, it comes from the Sanskrit word, the Self without a self. It is the mystical atom and the Divine Self in Sanskrit. The *Atman* is *Brahman,* the absolute being. The Divine ego is selfless; it lifts you up. It has no seed (*Sabhij*) to require you to come back to earth. If you are absorbed (*Laya*) in that it is *Nirbij,* without seed.

Aum: Is the first sound that came out of the ocean, which came out of *Brahman's* egg. Letters are alive. But the word did not come in the beginning at all, just a letter representing the sound, which the Indians say is the OM (or *Aum*).

Ayurveda: The science of life, treating the conditions of life and also promoting the profound knowledge of longevity.

Beta, Bet: The second letter in the Hebrew alphabet.

Bhagavad Gita: The scripture on yoga related by *Lord Krishna,* an incarnation of *Lord Vishnu.*

Bhagavatam: The Supreme Lord.

Bindu: Truth, the point of emergence and absorption of creation. The point is always in the center, the center of the heart.

Brahmacharya: A yogic practice to "always think of God" to a certain extent in life until acquiring knowledge and a control over the senses. To practice celibacy, in this sense, is to live in the consciousness of God, of the Creator.

Brahman: The absolute, unfathomable, one without a second; ever expanding; it was not even space, not even time.

Brahmanda: The egg of *Brahma,* the Creator; a bubble formed, the egg of *Brahman.* He and She were one. The energy was one.

Brahmarpanam Brahma Havir Brahma Gnou Brahmana Hutam Brahaiva Tena Gantavyam Brahma Karma Samadhina: A grace before taking food, translated as: *Brahman* (the Supreme) is the oblation, *Brahman* is the offering, *Brahman* is the One sacrificing Itself in Its own fire, verily *Brahman* is reached only by the one who always sees *Brahman* in action.

Brahmins: The priest class of India.

Brasad: To expand.

Buddhavidya: The science of mind and the science of elements.

Dharma: The universal law governing the universe and human life. The *dharma* is the adamantine justice that coordinates all elements by the one principle of truth, faith, and reverence. At the command of *dharma*, all cosmic energies are harnessed.

Dhyana: A term for meditation; the awareness that "in giving, we receive."

Dhrti: Bold-heartedness, with patience and fortitude.

Durachara: Bad conduct, which may turn into an enemy in the body and hurt the individual and the universal.

Ekarchitta: The mind (*ekarchitta*) can be at one point, which doesn't move but expands and contracts.

Gopala Krishna: A name for the *Lord Krishna* as a young cowherd boy in Vrindavan.

Gulab jamun: A famous Indian sweet of deep fried dumplings in a rose-scented syrup.

Guru: The light giver is the one who guides the spiritual aspirant on the path to awakening.

Hari: A name of *Lord Krishna*, meaning "to scrape."

Hridaya: The heart of God is a mysterious, classified secret of God.

Hirianyagarbha: The name for the aspect of the Creator Brahma, with the golden womb, He who has a belly full of gold.

Isha Upansihad 9th stanza proclaims:

Andham tamah praviśanti ye'vidyāmupāsate
tato bhūya iva te tamo ya u vidyāyām ratāh

The meaning is, "Those who worship the illusory pursuits and rites of the world remain enmeshed in the blinding darkness of ignorance. But into denser darkness enter those who are engrossed in the intellectual or psychological pursuits of knowledge for its own sake." The two movements on the path of evolution in relation to human beings are: the movement of outgoing and the movement of incoming or returning. These in Sanskrit are the *Pravritti Marga* or the involutionary path and the *Nivritti Marga* or the evolutionary path. The involution into matter leads to illusion and ignorance.

Japa: A spiritual practice of saying the names of God.

Kaayena Wachaa Manasendri Yairwaa, Budhyatamanaava Prakriti Swabhavaatth
    Whatever I do physically, whatever I do with work and through all senses
Karomi Yad Yad SaKakalam Parasmai, Naarayanaa Yeti Samrpayaam I
    Through natural instincts I offer all to you, great One, my defects, my all –
    You take care of it. Anything I do with body and mind, I offer all to You my Lord
    (One always does good things when offering to God – holiest of holies.)
    Above is translation of a mantra to assist in surrendering to the highest Principle)

Kakulagislaletomeklometali: Seven million years ago the human being was burnt by the eye of *Kakulagislaletomeklometali,* a sage. The ego entered the psyche and cannot be disciplined. It doesn't know what it is doing!

Karma Bhumi: Another name for the earth, the land of action.

Kumbakarna: The brother of the ferocious demon Ravenna, who worshiped Vishnu and was saved.

Jivatma: Is the oversoul that blesses.

Laya: Absorption (absorption is devotion)

Lord Krishna: The beloved Lord in Hinduism, an incarnation of *Lord Vishnu,* the principle of preservation.

Mahabharata: A great epic of Hindu literature, which houses the *Bhagavad Gita,* the scripture on yoga related by *Lord Krishna,* an incarnation of *Lord Vishnu.*

Mahda: Pride, one of the six enemies of the Self, when the ego rises and we do not distinguish it from the Divine Self. The other enemies are *Kama* (carnal passion), *Krodha* (anger, wrath), *Loha* (covetousness), *Moha* (madness, intoxication), and *Matsaya* (jealousy, envy).

Mantram: (Sanskrit, plural of *Mantra*) Come from seed roots of sound. The repetition of sacred seed sounds and names employed in many religious paths. Sacred sounds serve to awaken the body and mind into a more harmonious alignment with the central axis of the Core Self. Not invented, they are revelations from the Divine. Every Mantra has a particular healing energy associated with cosmic principles of formation through sound. The syllables, words, and intonations work on the cellular and subatomic levels. Working from the inside out, they restore potentiality and rearrange cosmic matter.

Mantra: Sacred sound combinations that save one who meditates on its significance; the paramount practice in this Dark Age.

Mara: Name of the evil one.

Maya: The cosmic illusion of separateness from the Source.

Moksha (liberation) or *Mukti:* There you completely dissolve in what you call God.

Nirbij: Without seed.

Nivritti Marga: The evolutionary path.

Nux Moschata: A homeopathic remedy that "puts your present consciousness in a stupor, then you remember the other, the wakefulness."

Pralhadha: Reabsorption of the universe or the deluge.

Panduranga: The name of God or *Vishnu* taken by the saint *Tukaram.*

Paramatman: The origin of oceanic bliss experienced by all newborn babies.

Pranams: A respectful salutation or reverential bowing, usually before a shrine or a deity, or to a revered person such as an elder or teacher or *guru.*

Purusha: The supreme human being.

Prakriti: Nature, with all its material elements and components.

Pratyahara: Detachment from sensory experience.

Pravritti Marga: The involutionary path.

Puranas: Not considered exactly scriptures, the epic teaching tales of humans and gods in Hindu literature.

Rabindra: Means the "king of light."

Radha: Considered a human incarnation of *Lakshmi* or *Vishnu's* consort, the name of the human consort of *Lord Krishna.*

Ram: Name of God as the incarnation of *Lord Vishnu* in the *Ramayana.*

Rasgula: A famous Indian sweet of soft cheese dumplings soaked in sugar syrup.

Ravenna: The ferocious demon who abducted *Sita,* and was slayed by her divine husband Ram, an incarnation of Vishnu.

Rishis: Are the great sages in between all the kinds of beings, gods, demons and humans. They maintain the order of the Supreme Law. They control the world, and creation is engineered through them by the Divine Bliss of God.

Sabhij: Seed(s) in the person that require the individual to come back to earth.

Sadchara: Good conduct.

Sadhasaviveka: Discernment, the discriminating power of the mind to differentiate the real from the unreal.

Sadhus: Holy men.

Sanctum Sanctorum: The holiest of the holies, from whence arises the actual energy of creation.

Sanyama: The term in Sanskrit for how we are ruined if we go on indulging in too many sensual activities.

Sarasvati: The goddess of knowledge.

Satsang: Gathering of truth seekers.

Shakti: The power of pure consciousness. *Shakti* is supreme power and must be joined to *Shiva,* pure consciousness. The core of *Shakti,* Nature, or *Prakriti* is darkness. *(Ma) Shakti* is this power as Mother.

Shiva: Pure consciousness. The core of *Shiva* is Light. The core of the human being is Light, is Spirit. *Shiva* is pure consciousness, and *Shakti* is the power of pure consciousness.

Shiva Shakti: The totality that created the original split as a compassionate act on the part of the combined forces of creation involved in each other as male and female, yin and yang, or *Prakriti* and *Purusha.*

Shristhi Stiti Laya: The creation, existence in time and space, and absorption of existence. You have a position. You position yourself as a human being. Then the absorption, *Laya,* is not destruction but absorption, going to the core.

Sthitaprajna: To be established in the Self; to be established in your Self is to establish in self-awareness.

Svayambhu: It formed itself … it is caused by itself. Nobody else caused it, caused by itself. *Svayambhuva* means "it became itself."

Tantra Shastra: A scripture instructing the human being to be enjoined in romance with the deity. In this sublimation, the person mates with the Divine principle, where at that stage one is not distracted by the male or female partner. Dr. Shyam warns that some *Tantriks* (practitioners of *Tantra* or *Kundalini Yoga*) and *Sheiks* spoiled *Kundalini Yoga.* This libido is the *Kundalini* rooted in the *Muladhara* chakra (root chakra at the base of the spine). The *Kunda* is the pit at the base of the spinal cord where the serpent power resides in three coils. When we give it a push through the breath, it rises through the central channel, the *Shushumna.* Knowing how to raise this energy, then we are not lost in the dungeon of the world. The energy is pushed upward and goes to the brain, where the mind is illuminated. When the *Kundalini* energy rises in the central *Shushumna,* the central channel in the spinal cord, then the brain becomes universal. It belongs to everyone and whoever comes near will be changed. If the *Muladhara* chakra is not active, the sex drive becomes active. Sex only gives a sense of relief by the release of instinctual energy. In real *Tantra*, the energy rises to the point of absorption in cosmic consciousness.

Tao: The unknowable, unthinkable, and untouchable.

Udhava Gita: The final scripture between *Lord Krishna* and his disciple *Udhava*.

Vasanas: Positive or negative traces or tendencies, which can be reawakened and influence desires and behavior.

Vayu: The god or principle of the wind and air.

Vihara: Right Recreation; part of Dr. Shyam's trinity of right conduct.

Vishnu: Supreme God, one of the trinity, assigned to the preservation of the universe; the sustainer incarnated as *Lord Ram* and *Lord Krishna*

Vishnu Murti: A consecrated statue of *Vishnu*

Yama: The god of death and of the *Dharma*, which is the universal law governing the cosmos and human life.

Printed in the United States
By Bookmasters